Anonymous

A Complete and Faithful Collection of the Several Papers

which have been published in Oxford - on the subject of subscription to

the XXXIX Articles, required from young persons at their matriculation

Anonymous

A Complete and Faithful Collection of the Several Papers
which have been published in Oxford - on the subject of subscription to the XXXIX Articles, required from young persons at their matriculation

ISBN/EAN: 9783337139544

Printed in Europe, USA, Canada, Australia, Japan

Cover: Foto ©Andreas Hilbeck / pixelio.de

More available books at **www.hansebooks.com**

A COMPLETE and FAITHFUL

COLLECTION

OF THE

SEVERAL PAPERS

WHICH HAVE BEEN

PUBLISHED IN OXFORD,

ON THE SUBJECT OF

Subscription to the XXXIX Articles,

Required from Young Persons at their

Matriculation.

OXFORD:

Printed, and Sold by the Booksellers in that University,
and at CAMBRIDGE; and by S. LEACROFT,
opposite Spring-Gardens, Charing Cross, LONDON.
M DCC LXXII.

ADVERTISEMENT.

THE following Sheets contain a faithful Collection of the several Papers which have hitherto been circulated in this Place on the Subject of Subscription to the XXXIX Articles. As it is probable that this Matter may be still farther agitated elsewhere, it is apprehended that the present Collection will not be unacceptable to the Public. If any other Papers should appear, they will be published as an Appendix.

OXFORD, *April* 20. 1772.

A COLLECTION
OF
PAPERS, &c.

No. I.

Origin of Subscription to the 39 Articles at Matriculation in the University of Oxford.

Ex Regift. Convoc. KK. p. 338.

Anno Domini 1581. Domino Roberto Comite
Anno Reginæ 23. Leyceſtriæ, Canc.
D^e James, Vice-Canc.
M^o Crane. M^o Madocks, Proc.
Novembris 2.

SECUNDO *Novembris in celebri convocatione magiſtrorum regentium et non regentium habita, lectæ erant literæ ab inſigniſſimo comite Leyceſtriæ cancellario noſtro ad venerabilem convocationem hoc exemplo ſubſcriptæ.*

" AND

" AND after my right hearty Commendations, as often heretofore, so now by late Complaints am I caused again to write unto you for Reformation, of divers Disorders amongst you, both in matters of Religion, in the Exercises of Learning, and in Apparel and sum other Pointes concerning Conversation. The Particulars are long to rehearce unto you, but may appear by a Scedule inclosed *, wherein the Faults and such Orders, as upon the present I could think convenient for Redress of them are set down together, I heartily and very earnestly pray you upon perusing the said Orders,

---

* *Imprimis*, That whereas the old Order of Matriculation is that within Six Days of every Scholar's first coming to Oxford, he shall take an Oath to observe the Statutes of this University, &c. and for as much as by the negligence and carelessness of many Heads, this hath been and daily is omitted, in so much that many Scholars have lived here a long Time being never registered in the University Booke, nether at any Time heretofore sworne to the said University, and by this Means many Papists have heretofore and may hereafter lurke among You, and be brought up by corrupt Tutors nether yelding to God nor to her Majestie or your University theare bounden Dutie as hath of late Yeares too much appeared and is evident in sundry younge Students in your Universitie, sum being atte Rome, sum in the Seminaries and other Places, all out of her Majesties Obedience, I have thought good to have this Order following to be established.

. First, that no Scholler be admitted into any College or Hall of the Universitie, unless he first before the Vice-Chancellor subscribe to the Articles of Religion agreed upon, take the Oathe of the Queens Majestie Supremacy, sweare to observe the Statutes of the Universitie if he be of lawfull Yeares to take an Othe and have his Name registred

in

Orders, if they shall be found such as in all Pointes you like of, that you will take farder Orders forthwith for the due and strict Observation of them, and if upon Consideration they shall not seem fit unto you for the Purpose and time, then that you will out of Hand add diminish alter and change for new any Thing that shall mislike, and setting down the same in such sort as in your own Judgement you shall think most fit, to see them likewise severely and throughly executed and observed that so the Disorders and Complaints of them may both ceace together, which I heartily wish, and

in the Matriculation Boke, which is by Statute as I heare to remaine with the Chancellour or Vice-Chancellour, and have a Note under the Vice-Chancellour's Hand that he hath done the Premisses, and the Head of the College or Hall of which he shall be, or some of the Deanes and Censors doe at some convenient Time signifie the said Othe. and Subscription to the whole Company.

Secondly, That for as much as sundry Parents being themselves Recusants, or knowne or suspected Papists, have sent their Sonns to the Universitie and dayley doe, and are desirous to have their Sonns by all Likelyhood trayned up in the same Religion, and for that Purpose have as it may appear certaine select Tutors among you, of whome at the least they hope well to have their Children instructed after their owne Desire, I have thought good also to wish that by Act of Convocation it may be likewise established that noe Tutor hereafter be allowed, but such as be of sound Religion, and that under the Hand of the Vice-Chancellor for the Time being, and three Doctors of Div. and 3 Bach. of Div. or three Preachers for that Purpose assembled all togeather where it shall please the Vice-Chancellor.

Thirdly, &c.

so desiring to hear speedily from you what you shall do herein I bid you heartily farewell. From the Court the 5th of October 1581—Your very Friend

R. LEYCESTER."

" *Quibus literis lectis statim proponitur convocationi quædam tam ad statuta nostræ Univerfitatis observanda quam de juramento supremæ regiæ majestratis suscipiendo per omnes Scholares maturæ Ætatis priusquam in Collegia sive Aulas admittantur, tum etiam ut publicæ lectiones in singulis facultatibus diligenter observentur, quæ omnia et singula prout publicè perlecta erant in convocatione sic suo ordine subscribuntur.*"

The several Articles mentioned in the Schedule being read in the Convocation the Vice-Chancellor added three more Proposals, and then nominating Delegates to consider of them, they framed these * Decrees following from them.

" *Novembris* 14° *A. D.* 1581.

" *In solenni Convoc. Doct^m Magⁿ Reg^m et non Reg. Decimo quarto Nov. habitâ leges subscriptæ publice perlectæ et Communi omnium consensu approbatæ et sancitæ sunt.*

" *Imprimis.*

---

* Ex. Reg. KK. fol. 340, 341.

"*Imprimis.* It is decreed that no Student being of the Age of 16 or upwards and unmatriculated being already admitted into any College or Haule of this Univerſitie, ſhall theare any longer abide then the Friday ſennight after the Publication hereof unleſs he have under the Vicechancellours Hand for the Time being a Certificate of his Subſcription both to the Articles of Religion, her Majeſties Supremacy, and alſo to obſerve the Orders and Statutes of this Univerſity, and have his Name regeſtred in the Matriculation Booke.

"*Item,* that no Student hereafter to be admitted ut ſupra ſhall longer ſtay than till the next Friday ſennight after his Admiſſion unleſs he perform all Things in ſuch Sort as are above ſpecified: Except the ſaid Scholler or Student either now being or hereafter to be admitted be not full 16 Yeares of Age, but being between 12 and 16 he ſhall but ſubſcribe and be matriculat, and being under 12, he ſhall be matriculat onelye, and ſo continue till he or they be of Years ſufficient to performe the reſt above ſpecified. Provided alwayes that the ſaid Student or Scholler that is to performe any thing that is above ſpecified ſhall attend upon Frydayes in Terme Time at the Vicechancellours Court, and at all other Times at his Lodging.

"*Item,*

" *Item*, That if the Head of any Colledge or Haule, or in his Abſence the ſenior or Vice Head or Governour, doe ſuffer in his Houſe any Student or Scholler by him admitted not performing the Thinges above ſpecified, he ſhall forfeit Twenty Shillinges and the Scholler 40 s. for every Weeke *toties quoties*.

" *Item*, That all private Tutors or Readers hereafter, ſhall be allowed by the Conſent of the Vice-Chancellour, the Head of the ſame Houſe whereof he or they ſhall be, and alſo the Conſent of 2 Doct. of Devinitye or two Preachers at the leaſt—And that no Tutor or Reader now beeing that is or ſhall be by Othe detected of vehement ſuſpicion of Popery ſhall after the Nativ. of Xt. next inſuinge retain any Pupill or Scholler, unleſs he doe, being thereunto required, purge himſelf before the Vice-Chancellour and Proctors by his own Othe or the Hands of three Preachers in the Univerſitie."

Extract from the preſent Statutes of the Univerſity, compiled in the Year 1616.

Tit. II. §. 3. " Quotquot autem in Matriculam Univerſitatis redigendi accedunt, ſi decimum ſextum ſuæ ætatis annum attigerint, Articulis fidei & Religionis ſubſcribant; & de agnoſcendo primatu Regiæ Majeſ-

Majeſtatis, nec non de fidelitate Univerſitati exhibenda, ac Satutis, Privilegiis, & conſuetudinibus ejuſdem obſervandis, juxta formam hactenus uſitatam, corporale juramentum præſtent.

" Quod ſi infra decimum ſextum & ſupra duodecimum ætatis annum extiterint, Articulis fidei & Religionis duntaxat ſubſcribent, & in Matriculam redigentur.

" Quod ſi duodecimum non excelſerint, in Matriculam duntaxat referentur; utrique tamen poſtmodo, ubi ad maturam ætatem pervenerint, quâ cætera requiſita præſtare poſſint, tum demum ea præſtare teneantur ſub pœna non ſiſtentium ſe Matriculandos."

Tit. III. §. 2. " Tutor vero Scholares Tutelæ & regimini ſuo commiſſos probis moribus imbuat, & in probatis authoribus inſtituat; & maxime in rudimentis Religionis & doctrinæ Articulis in ſynodo *Lond.* (anno 1562.) editis: ac pro virili ſuo, diſciplinæ in Eccleſia Anglicana publicè receptæ eos conformes præſtabit. Quod ſi quis in aliquo prædictorum deliquerit, arbitrio Cancellarii vel Vice-Cancellarii coerceatur."

Commencement of Subscription to the three Articles in the 36th Canon.

An. } Dom. 1616.
{ 14 Jacobi.

* It being insinuated to the King what Dangers would proceed by the training up of yong Students in grounds of Puritanisme and Calvinisme, if some Directions did not issue out from his Majestie for the Course of their Studies, and that there was no readier Way to advance the Presbyterial Government in this Kingdom than by suffering yong Scholers to be seasoned with Calvinian Doctrines, and that for want of Subscription to the three Articles contained in the 36th Canon, not only Lecturers, but divers other Preachers in & about the Universitie, positively maintained such Points of Doctrine as were not maintained or allowed by the Church of England. He therefore having taken these Things into consideration, did by the Advice of such Bishops and others of the Clergy as were then about him, dispatch upon the 18th of January these † Directions following to the Vicechancellor, certain Heads of Houses, the two Professors of Divinity & the two Proctors

───────────

* Hist. & Antiq. Univ. Oxon. A. Wood P. 322. & MSS. Hist. P. 736.   † Reg. Convoc. N. fo. 32. a & b.

Proctors of the University to be carefully and speedily put in execution.

" JAMES REX.

" 1. His Majesty signified his Pleasure that he would have all that take any Degree in Schooles to subscribe to the three Articles.

" 2. That no Preacher be allowed to preach in the Town but such as be every Way conformable both by Subscription and every other Way.

" 3. That, &c."

In consequence of the above Directions a Convocation was holden on the 12th of Feb. 1616, in which " * Procuratores no-
" minabant hos egregios viros ad deliberan-
" dum, et statuendum de quibusdam ad
" Directiones regias propositas spectantibus,
" nec non, &c.
    " viz. Doctorem Goodwin
    " ------ Prideaux, &c. &c."

On the last Day of March 1617, the Decrees of the above Delegates were read and approved in Convocation. The first of which is as follows: " Forma subscribendi ab omnibus graduum Academicorum Candidatis diligenter observanda Hujusmodi

---

* Reg. Convoc. N. fol. 36. b.

modi perpetua esto---Ego A. perlectis prius vel ab alio coram me recitatis orthodoxæ fidei et Religionis Articulis 39, et in sacrâ Synodo Londini habitâ A. D. 1562 constabilitis, simulque tribus Capitibus in aliâ Synodo Londinensi sub annum 1604 decretis et in canone 36 * redactis, sciens volensque ex animo subscribo.----Præsentationis etiam in Domo Congregationis coram Domino Pro-Cancellario et Procuratoribus solennis formula hæc adhibetor---Præsento vobis hunc meum B. vel S. ut admittatur &c. ad quam quidem admissionem scio eum aptum

---

* *Three Articles of the* 36*th Canon.*

I. That the King's Majesty under God, is the only Supreme Governour of this Realm, and of all other his Highnesses Dominions and Countrys, as well in all Spiritual or Ecclesiastical things or causes, as Temporal; and that no Foreign Prince, Person, Prelate, State or Potentate, hath, or ought to have, any Jurisdiction, Power, Superiority, Preeminence or Authority, Ecclesiastical or Spiritual, within his Majesty's said Realms, Dominions and Countrys.

II. That the Book of Common Prayer, and of Ordering of Bishops, Priests, and Deacons, containeth in it nothing contrary to the Word of God, and that it may lawfully so be used, and that I myself will use the Form in the said Book prescribed in publick Prayer, and Administration of the Sacraments, and none other.

III. That I allow the Book of Articles of Religion agreed upon by the Archbishops and Bishops of both Provinces and the whole Clergy in the Convocation holden at *London* in the Year of our Lord God, One thousand five hundred sixty and two; and that I acknowledge all and every the Articles therein contained, being in number Nine and thirty, besides the Ratification, to be agreeable to the Word of God,

aptum habilem et idoneum moribus et Scientiâ. Quem infuper fcio legiffe vel ab alio recitatos audiviffe omnes Articulos quibus coram procuratoribus fubfcripfit."——
Reg. Convoc. N. Fol. 41. a & b.

No. II.

The Case of Subscription to the Thirty-nine Articles, required of all Scholars matriculated in the University of Oxford. Stated and considered.

THE two Universities were instituted as Places of Education for the Youth of this Kingdom, to qualify them for the Service of their Country, in Church and State, as by Law established.

The Nature and Design of their Institution, the Statutes which are founded upon it, and the established Modes of Discipline to be observed in them, do evidently prove, that they were intended only for the Education of Members of the Church of England.

That no Papist, or Sectary of any Kind, might gain an Admission into this University, the Wisdom of our Protestant Ancestors thought it expedient, for the greater Security of this reformed Church as by Law established, to provide a Test of the Religious Principles of the Persons to be admitted into it.

This Test, which has been required and submitted to for near Two hundred Years, consists

consists in a Subscription to the Thirty-nine Articles, which contain the Doctrines of the Church of England. And all Persons of Twelve Years of Age are required to subscribe to them at their Matriculation.

The Question is, Whether this Test ought to be *retained*, or *abrogated*, or *altered?*

If it be totally *abrogated*, the Constitution, Order, and Discipline of the University will be fundamentally changed. It will be laid open to Persons of all Religious Persuasions, who will be at Liberty to act agreeably to their Persuasions, so far at least as they can plead Conscience in their Behalf. If any one cannot conscientiously join in the Service of the Church, he will say, that it would be wicked in *Him* to violate his Conscience, and in *You* to require it. Thus the University will become a Seminary of Schism, which it was designed to prevent; and will put Arms into the Hands of Persons, who will use them offensively against the Established Church, which their Institution requires them to guard and defend.

If the Test be proposed to be *altered*, it will be right first to consider, Whether any such Objection may be made to it, as may not be removed to the Satisfaction of every candid and reasonable Mind.

No

No Man of Common Senſe can think, that a Subſcription to the Articles required of Perſons who have attained the Twelfth Year of their Age, can be meant to require a formal and explicit Aſſent to the Senſe of the Doctrines contained in them, when they are not ſo much as required to have read them; or that it carries in it an Obligation that they ſhould never diſſent from any of them, ſhould they hereafter ſee Reaſon for it, when they ſhould have Abilities to underſtand and judge of them. It never meant any more, nor was it ever underſtood to mean any more, than that it was a Declaration of the Perſon ſubſcribing, that he was a Member of the Church of England, and, as ſuch, would conform to the Worſhip and Diſcipline of it. All that he is ſuppoſed to know of the Doctrines is, that they are the Doctrines of the Church, of which he has been educated a Member; and that for the preſent, he acquieſces in them as ſuch, ſuſpending any farther Judgment of them, till he ſhall be better able to examine them.

All this the matriculated Youth may very well underſtand, and ſubmit to with a ſafe Conſcience; it requiring no more than a Perſuaſion, which he certainly brings with him, that the Church he has been educated in has no Deſign to impoſe upon him, or lead him aſtray.

If any Thing more is requifite to put this Matter in its true Light, in which it has been feen and approved for Two Centuries paft, by as learned, religious, and confcientious Men as ever lived, let an Explanation of this Kind be inferted in the Statute Book, in the fame Manner as the Epinomis of Bifhop Saunderfon is, in refpect to the Oath of Obligation to obferve the Penal Statutes.

If fuch an Explanation is not fatisfactory, and fome Teft is ftill thought neceffary at the Time of Matriculation, to be required by the Univerfity, in Conformity to the Defign and Nature of its Inftitution, What other Teft can be propofed? I can think but of Two Ways of *Subftitution*.

The one is, That the young Scholar be required to make a *Declaration* that he is a Member of the Church of England; and that he will conform, during his Refidence in it, to the Rules and Difcipline of it, as by Law eftablifhed.

The other is, That his Tutor fhall ftipulate for him, in the above-mentioned Particulars.

As to the former, I fee no Difference betwixt the Mode of *Declaration*, and that of *Subfcription*, as before explained.

As to the latter, the *Declaration* or *Subfcription* muft be as obligatory upon the Pupil, as if they were made by himfelf; otherwife,

otherwife, they have no Meaning at all, but muft be downright Chicanery and Prevarication.

Degrees, in the ordinary Difpenfation of them, were never intended to be beftowed by the Univerfity but upon Members of the Church of England; no other Perfons being capable of being Members of the Univerfity. Thofe indeed, who are capable of Degrees, are fuppofed to have read its Articles, and to underftand the Doctrines of them. And if any one thinks that any of them are not reconcileable, by a fair and reafonable Interpretation, to the effential Faith of a Chriftian, though he may be an outward Conformift, he is, in Truth, no real Member of the Church of England as by Law eftablifhed. And this he declares, if he witholds his Subfcription to them. But before the Univerfity can difpenfe with his Subfcription, a new Mode of Proceeding muft be enjoined by legal Authority. Otherwife, it will be either a tacit Acknowledgment on the Part of the Univerfity, that the long-eftablifhed Subfcription is indefenfible, or that it muft no longer be confidered as a Seminary for Members of the Church of England only.

And even fuppofing that our Articles want Revifal, Explanation, or Amendment, (which, whenever it is attempted, muft be

the

the Work of very wife and learned Men, performed with great Caution and Circumfpection) why is it expected, that the Univerfity fhould take the Lead in fatisfying the Scruples of the prefent Times? Why are not their Confciences to be refpected as much as other Peoples? And if this Univerfity is perfuaded, that no *Alteration* ought to be made in the prefent Teft, but what will leave the Purport and Meaning of it juft the fame as it now is, and that the total *Abrogation* of it is abfolutely inconfiftent with the very Nature and Defign of its Inftitution, it is nugatory to require the one, and muft be unreafonable and unjuft to require the other.

And what End will this Abrogation anfwer? The Attack upon the Univerfity Subfcription, is an Attack only upon the Outworks of the Fortrefs; if thefe are gained, will not the Acquifition encourage a more furious Attack upon the Citadel? If the Church of England ftands at prefent upon a good Foundation, let it be vigoroufly defended by all who confider it as the Bulwark of the Reformation; and let us hope, that our Superiors will be careful that no Alterations be made in it, if any Alterations are expedient, but fuch as will give it an additional and real Security,

curity, Strength and Reputation, leaving it in Poffeffion of the effential Doctrines and Conftitution of a truly Primitive, Chriftian, and Apoftolical Church.

Dr. J— tie.

No. III.

Considerations on the Expediency of making some Alteration in regard to the present Mode of Subscribing to the XXXIX *Articles in this University.*

THERE is no Occasion to inquire into the original Design of the Institution of the Universities: it is sufficient for our Purpose to know, that the present Mode of Subscription to the Thirty-nine Articles was injoined by an University Statute, made at the Instance of our Chancellor, Lord *Leicester*.

It is agreed that this University was intended, by the said Statute, as a Seminary not of Learning only, but also of the Protestant Religion, as by Law established.

It is also agreed, that some Test is necessary from Persons entering as Members of the same: since their religious Opinions cannot be Matter of Indifference to the well being of such a Seminary.

The present Test is Subscription to the Thirty-nine Articles: and this Test, it is acknowledged, has been required and submitted to, for near two Hundred Years.

I will go farther, and add, that I wish

it might have continued without Impeachment for many Hundred Years more.

But suppoſing any untoward and unexpected Emergency to ariſe; is this Teſt, in it's preſent identical Form, to be neceſſarily and uniformly retained, without Limitation or Alteration, in all Times, and under all Circumſtances whatſoever? So ſay ſome, and here we muſt part.

The Neceſſity of the Times gave Riſe to this Teſt; the ſame Neceſſity may oblige us to diſpenſe with ſome of it's Forms. The venerable Sanction of Antiquity is a Recommendation in their favour; the Concurrence of wiſe, learned, and judicious Perſons, who have lived before us, is an additional Recommendation. But as no Legiſlators, on the one Hand, can foreſee what Emendations in any Inſtitution Time may render abſolutely requiſite; ſo, on the other Hand, Limitations and Amendments may be introduced, without any Reflection upon the Virtue and good Senſe of our Predeceſſors. The *pregnant Principle of Neceſſity* may be urged upon this Occaſion with much greater Force, than in a late political Controverſy; and if the Conſideration of mere Antiquity is to overrule this Plea, Popery will ſtep in with her *Petition of Grievances*, and will claim to be heard.

The *Abrogation* of a Teſt, to be required of Perſons matriculated, is out of the Queſtion;

tion; the Alteration of it is all that is here infifted on; and even this only in Confideration of the powerful Spirit of Oppofition to the prefent Mode of Subfcription. This Spirit it is not in our power to controul, we have nothing to do therefore but to blunt it's Edge by prudent Anticipation.

At the Time when the late Petition met with it's deferved Repulfe in the Houfe of Commons, the Friends of this Univerfity immediately expreffed their Wifhes, that fome Alteration might be adopted, refpecting the Bufinefs of Subfcription to Articles: Thofe wifhes are ftill preffed upon us from every Quarter; and the more fo, as our beft Friends not only think fome Alterations fafe and practicable, but further are well affured, that unlefs we voluntarily comply, we fhall be compelled to fubmit upon difadvantageous Conditions.

Thus far, upon the Prefumption that nothing plaufible can be urged in Favour of an Alteration, and that the fole Motive for making Conceffions is the Spirit of Faction, and the perfevering Temper of a difappointed Party.

But can nothing popular, I will not fay reafonable, be advanced againft the received Practice; chiefly in regard to young Perfons at Matriculation? In whatever Light *we* confider it, it appears in rather an unfavourable one to thofe at a Diftance. They
esteem

esteem the Age of twelve Years as too early a Period to require Subscription: Subscription they think implies an unfeigned assent to the Doctrines and Tenets therein contained; many of which, by reason of their tender and inexperienced Age, young Men are absolutely incapable of understanding. To require it therefore they think highly unreasonable, and unworthy a learned and respectable Body. Yet is such Assent supposed by the Generality to be really given; no explanatory Rule being laid down by Authority, to justify either an express or a mental reservation; and he that should say that he subscribed without believing, or thinking it was required of him to believe, what he had subscribed, would lay himself open to the Charge of Prevarication. This Charge is continually thrown into the Teeth of such Subscribers in the Church, by the Dissenters; and it must be owned, the Heathen Maxim of old does not sound very creditably in the Mouth of a Christian Teacher,

Linguâ juravi, mentem injuratam gero.

But what says the Defender of this notable Salvo? " No Man of Sense can think " that Subscription to Articles, required of " Persons who have attained the twelfth " Year of their Age, can be meant to re- " quire a formal and explicit Assent to the " Doctrines contained in them.—It never
" meant,

"meant, nor was it ever underſtood to
"mean, any more than that it was a De-
"claration of the Perſon ſubſcribing, that
"he was a Member of the Church of
"England; and as ſuch, would conform
"to the Worſhip and Diſcipline of it."
This is boldly ſaid, and certainly wants
Proof; at leaſt, I know ſome very reſpectable Perſons in this Place, who have not yet
Common Senſe enough to ſee this Truth;
unleſs perhaps till now when they are hap-
pily thus better informed. However, I will
cloſe with the Writer of the *Caſe*, *&c.*
upon this Footing; and if by the preſent
Mode of Subſcription, required of Perſons
of twelve Years of Age, be meant no more
than ſuch a Declaration, where can be the
Harm of ſubſtituting ſuch a Declaration in
the room of ſuch Subſcription? *All* may
not be poſſeſſed of the ſame non-diſtinguiſhing Faculty with this Writer in the
preſent Caſe: *He* confeſſes them to be one
and the ſame thing: *He* therefore can have
no reaſonable Objection; they who think
them different, may by this Exchange have
their Objections removed. Whether this
would not be a more open and liberal Method of Proceeding, than by a formal *Epinomis*, under Sanction of the Univerſity,
declaring that by Subſcription to Articles,
the young Men are not expected to give
their Aſſent to the Poſitions contained in
them,

them, let the unprejudiced determine. Besides will any Man of Senfe ferioufly affirm, that the Univerfity might confiftently with common Prudence avowedly undertake, in thefe Times, by any new Statute, to explain away the Meaning of an Act of Parliament, fo as to elude the Force of it totally?

But, does the Writer really think there is no Difference between fubfcribing to the Articles, and declaring our Confent to the Worfhip and Difcipline of the Church of England? Is every Pofition, contained in the Articles, either expreffed or virtually implied in the Liturgy? And is Subfcription to thefe Articles the only Teft, that we are Members of the Proteftant Religion, as by Law eftablifhed in thefe Kingdoms? What becomes then of the Bulk of the People whofe Attendance on the Service of the Church of England may be exemplary, and their Conformity to the Liturgy fincere; and who neverthelefs never heard of the Articles? I beg leave therefore ftill to think not only that there is a wide Difference between fuch Declaration and fuch Subfcription, but that the Writer of the Cafe is of the fame Opinion. And if not; why this ftrenuous Oppofition to fuch a fubftituted Form? efpecially, as by the Conceffion we lofe nothing of the Effence, *ipfo confitente*; and by being unfeafonably tenacious, may

be

be treated, by those who wish us no good, as Lord Peter was treated by fanatical John, who not only stripped off the Lace, but tore the Coat into the Bargain. I wish these Apprehensions were ill-founded: It is a good Maxim, *Noli quieta turbare:* But the Signal is already given, and the Cry for Alteration is gone forth; the Question is, Whether we choose to capitulate, making our own Terms, or to surrender at Discretion.

I know that " Firmness" is the favourite Topic with some, and " that we have no-" thing to do but to sit still." But is it in our Power? And by being silent ourselves, can we stop the Mouths of our Opponents? Before we determine thus, we shall do well to look about, and estimate our Forces. The very Persons, who in the late Petition supported the Church, whisper in the Ear of the Universities, that our present Mode of Subscription, in all its Forms, is untenable Ground, and that unless we abandon it, they must desert us. If the Torrent is so prevalent, who would not wish to narrow our Fences, rather than have them thrown open to every Invader? For my own Part, I should be sorry to see the modelling of our Statutes, especially such as relate to Religious Restraints, in the Hands of any Parliament, not excepting the present.

E But,

"But, says the same Writer, before the University can dispense with Subscription, a new Mode of Proceeding must be enjoined by legal Authority. Otherwise, it will be a tacit Acknowledgment on the Part of the University, that the long established Subscription is indefensible, or that it must no longer be considered as a Seminary for Members of the Church of England only." But has not the Writer himself suggested a new Mode of Proceeding; I mean the Declaration above mentioned? And what does He mean by legal Authority? He cannot surely doubt of the legal Authority of the University to alter the Statutes made by itself. And if such Alteration be a tacit Acknowledgment that the present Mode is indefensible; what then? Is not a tacit Acknowledgment as reputable, in this Case, as an open One? For my Part, I shall never think it a Disgrace to acknowledge myself in an Error, much less to acknowledge that others might have erred before me; and, least of all, to acknowledge, that to preserve the Body we should do wisely to lop off a Limb. And supposing it true, that the University is a Seminary for the Members of the Church of England only; yet how do we enforce the contrary, by adopting the Declaration, the Essence of which is, Conformity to the Doctrine and Discipline of the Church of England?

Upon

Upon the Whole, I fee nothing formidable in the Propofal for an Alteration as above reftrained. But I tremble at the Confequences of an obftinate Perfeverance in the received Form: as by an ill-judged Firmnefs we may oblige our Superiors not only to exempt old as well as young from Subfcription, but to leave nothing to be fubfcribed by either in the Way of Subftitution.

OXFORD, March 19, 1772.

Dr. D

No. IV.

THE Design of the Author of *the Case of Subscription*, &c. was to vindicate the Establishment and Continuance of the present Mode of Subscription, upon the only Principle, as he apprehends, which can vindicate either. The Explanation upon which the Vindication rests is not his own: He received it from his Tutor, and always communicated it to his Pupils before their Matriculation.

He had Reason to suppose, that Persons abroad did not see the Thing in its true Light. He endeavoured to represent it in such a one, as might not only skreen the University from the Reproach of an absurd and arbitrary Conduct, in requiring from young People a formal Assent to the Truth of Propositions which they knew it was impossible for them to understand; but to undeceive those who might think, without further Reflection, that we required such an Assent. He knows his Attempt has satisfied some reasonable and respectable Men, who are Friends to the University.— He never expected it would satisfy its Enemies. He thought it might furnish an Argument of Defence to those who might be willing to favour us with their Protection,

Protection, by which a good Face at least might be put upon the Matter, and our Censurers might see, that our Practice was not so indefensible as they imagined.

He cannot possibly have any Objection to the projected Mode of *Declaration*, considered in itself, as he thought, and still thinks, that it does not at all differ from the present Mode of *Subscription* rightly understood; but there *may* be Objections to the Alteration considered in its Consequences.

The Attack upon our Subscription took its Rise from that which was made upon the whole Body of the Articles. The Church of England was not to be taken by *Storm*; our Adversaries have a Mind to see what they can do by *Sap*. They are first to get the University to acknowledge, that they have been very wrong in requiring from young Persons, at their Matriculation, an *Acquiescence* in, for I can never call it an *Assent* to, the Doctrines of the Church, into the Faith of which they were *baptized*. This will not satisfy. The next Step will be, to exempt all, who are to take Degrees, from the Obligation to subscribe the Articles, except perhaps, for the present, Degrees in Divinity; by which Means, Persons of any or no Religion, may have a Claim to the Honours of the University, in direct Contradiction

to

to the Nature of its Inftitution, and all the Principles of its Polity. The Senfe of the Univerfity will afterwards be brought as an Argument for totally abolifhing a Subfcription, which they have acknowledged to be indefenfible, as intolerable to the Confciences of *many*; and therefore is a Grievance that ought to be removed from the Confciences of *all* who feel the Weight of it. This Chain of Confequences is not improbable, if we confider the Principles and Defigns of our Reformers.

But what fhall we do with the Oath of Supremacy, which an Act of Parliament obliges *many* Perfons in this Place to take at the Age of eighteen Years, as the Univerfity Statute does *all* at the Age of fixteen Years? This has a powerful Sanction, and I fuppofe we do not intend to alter it. And yet I apprehend, that the *Oath* ftands in Need of the fame Grains of Allowance as the *Subfcription*. The young People, who are obliged to take it, *fwear* againft the Pope's Supremacy, in all Matters *Ecclefiaftical and Spiritual*, without knowing any Thing more about it than they do of the Articles.

If our Plea is a reafonable one, no reafonable Man will be *angry* for having had it offered to his Confideration. If mere prudential Reafons fhould preponderate in the Judgment of thofe who are well affected

to

to us, they ought to be communicated, and they will be duly attended to. But the Author of *the Cafe*, &c. thinks, that upon this Occafion we ought to fhew a proper Refpect to our Chancellor. — That as the Subfcription was eftablifhed upon the Recommendation of *one Chancellor*, it ought not to be cancelled but upon the Judgment and Recommendation of *another*.

D.^r J—kie.

No. V.

No. V.

THE sedate Author of "Confiderations on the Expediency of making fome Alteration," &c. feems to found his Arguments upon falfe Principles. His Fears make him forget what Ground he treads upon. "He trembles *at*" Things which *are not*, namely, "Confequences." He founds a Retreat, before He fees the Face of an Enemy. He flies, before any Man is ready to purfue; and that with fuch thoughtlefs Precipitation, as to leave Reafon far behind him; and neither to know, poor Man! wherefore, nor whither, he is running. He "agrees" however to the Truth of fome FACTS, which had been mentioned in the *Cafe ftated*, and then fays, he "will go farther, and add" to thefe Facts — what Fact? why, a WISH. — He afferts it to be "SUFFICIENT for our Purpofe to know that the prefent Mode of Subfcription to the thirty-nine Articles was injoined by an Univerfity Statute, made at the Inftance of our Chancellor, Lord Leicefter."—But He is by much too hafty in making this Affumption: For *Expediency* ought to be poftponed to *Right* and *Authority*. This Univerfity Statute, though made at the Inftance of our Chancellor Leicefter,

Leicester, was adopted into the subsequent Code, compil'd by Arch-Bishop Laud, and enacted by the *Joint-Authority* of the *Sovereign* and the *University*. It is ordain'd by the Statutes of this Code, that no Alteration shall be made in them, by any *inferior* Power to that, by which they were enacted: And every Member of our legislative Body is forbid upon Oath to consent to the making of any such Alteration. " Expediency" therefore, or which is the same Thing, " the Necessity of the Times, which gave Rise to this Test" of Subscription, cannot oblige us to dispense with any of it's Forms; because such Necessity, though a *sufficient* Motive to those, who had *Authority*, to *establish* these Forms, would be no Warrant to us, to *remove* any of them, who are under a *sacred Obligation* NOT " to *dispense* with them." " The pregnant Principle of Necessity" is in Truth pregnant with nothing else, but Mischief: It is oftentimes imaginary or fictitious: It is always the arbitrary *Substitute* of *Right*, and derives all it's Force from *Power:* It is deservedly excluded from every other but " *political* Controversy," and is unquestionably the worst of Answers that a Protestant could make to the pretended Plea of Priority of Right, or " the popish Petition of Grievances."

F   If

If many "Friends of the University have expressed their Wishes, that some Alteration might be adopted;" and "those Wishes are still pressed upon us from every Quarter;" it is surprizing, that many Persons resident in this University, whose Ears and Eyes are open to publick Occurrences, should never, before their reading of these Considerations, have received the Information. Suppose however the Truth of these *gratis Dicta:* and what Anticipation in our Part can be "*prudent*" enough to stop the Progress or assuage the Fury " of this powerful Spirit of Opposition?" Can the wary and provident Author of *Considerations* imagine, that, contrary to the Experience of antient and modern Times, the " Spirit of Faction" can be appeased by moderate " *Concessions?*" That the " persevering Temper of a disappointed Party" will voluntarily desist, before the *Dominion of Grace* is a second Time established in the *Ruin of Ordinances*; and the Spirit of Faction, *strengthened* by Concessions, is become superior to all Controll?

The Author's " plausible and popular" Arguments are unwarrantable and inconclusive. If the Expostulations of " those at a Distance" be, as he intimates they are, " *unreasonable*;" what Conclusions are to be deduced from them? Why does this grave and argumentative Writer obtrude
upon

upon the Notice of a learned University the Prattlings of such Infants in Argumentation? Why does He not rather admonish them in private to be modest and silent; till they can talk like Men; till they can utter Things *reasonable*, and worthy of the Attention of a learned and respectable Body? Why should he so much encourage their Vanity, as to repeat from them the Latin Sentences which they have learned by Heart, but know not how to apply? He ought to have taught them, that *jurare* signifies *to take an Oath*, not *to subscribe:* And further, that they certainly must mistake, if they suppose the Author of the *Case stated* to have suggested, that some Members of this University subscribe with their Hand, but *keep their Mind disengaged.* That elegant and rational Writer maintains, that young Persons of the Age of twelve subscribe to the Articles WITHOUT *mental Reservation:* That they declare for the present, that they are *bona fide* Members of the Church of England; and *do not reserve* in their Minds an *Intention* of separating from it's Worship and Discipline.— If there be any " respectable Persons in this Place," who " have not *yet*, unless till *now*, common Sense enough to see" the Difference between the Doctrine of the *Case stated* and the Representation given of it by the Author of *Considerations*, they must indeed

F 2   be

be " poſſeſſed of a non-diſtinguiſhing Faculty," and muſt derive their Reſpectability from other Endowments than thoſe of the Underſtanding.

The Writer of Conſiderations is a Perſon of very extraordinary Intelligence. He receives important Informations by private Whiſpers; and thinks too, that by a peculiar Faculty of Diſcernment He knows the Opinions of other Men, better than themſelves do. Thus he " modeſtly begs Leave to think," that the Author of the *Caſe ſtated* is of the " *ſame Opinion*" with the Author of *Conſiderations*; though he acknowledges concerning that ingenious Perſon, that he writes in Support of a contrary Opinion. Perhaps the learned Gentleman, thus injured, may do himſelf Juſtice: He may vindicate his *Honour*; though his *Arguments* do not ſeem to need a Vindication; but, it is probable, when attentively and impartially examined, will be generally approved. For though the " Coat of *Lord Peter* is ſtripped and torn;" there is not as yet any Hole to be found in the Coat of this honeſt *Martin:* And he will probably be able to preſerve it entire, and keep " *fanatical John*" at a proper Diſtance. At leaſt, He ſeems to be a Perſon of more Diſcernment, as well as Fortitude, than either to think that after " the Signal is given, he can capitulate upon his own

own Terms;" or, to take it for granted, that, if he waits the Affault, he fhall foon be *compelled* " *to furrender at Difcretion.*"

Courage, dear Sir; and pluck up your drooping Spirits. Pray, a little Chriftian Patience and manly Refolution! and rather let us be deferted by all our whifpering Friends, than ourfelves fly from our Advantage-Ground, and bafely defert our appointed Station. Confider, Sir, what great and unforefeen Advantages have fometimes accrued from " Firmnefs" and Perfeverance. So long as our prefent " Ground is tenable," let us not wilfully abandon it to any pert Invader. " The Torrent" may poffibly be diverted from it's prefent Courfe; or it may in Time fubfide, if we prudently *fupport* our " Fences:" But it furely is not the Seafon for tampering with the Fences, while the Waters rage: To " narrow" the Banks, would be a Work of Difficulty and Danger, to remove them would be Deftruction.

The Author of the *Cafe* has afferted, that the Subfcription of Perfons, who have attained the twelfth Year of their Age, " can mean no more, than that they are Members of the Church of England, and will conform to it's Worfhip," &c. Which the Confiderer feems to think equivalent to this Propofition, namely, that Declaration by Subfcription is *neceffary*; and is the *only* Thing

Thing neceffary to *conftitute* a Member of the Church eftablifhed. " Does the Author of the Cafe really think, fays he, that there is no Difference between fubfcribing to Articles, and declaring Affent to Worfhip," &c. that " Subfcription to the Articles is the *only* Teft," &c. " What then, fays he, becomes of the Bulk of the People, who never heard of the Articles?" That learned Writer does not feem, by what he has *faid*, to have *thought* any fuch Thing. The peculiar Subject of his Treatife is the Subfcription of *Members* of this *Univerfity*: He thinks it expedient that *all thefe* fhould declare themfelves Members of the *Church eftablifhed*; and that *Boys of twelve* Years of Age do make this, and *only* this, Declaration, by their Subfcription to the Articles. " The Bulk of the People" may be very good Churchmen, without Subfcription; and might be very bad ones with it: But they are neither under the Authority of this *Univerfity*, nor under the Author's Confideration: And He is too accurate a Writer to intermix Impertinencies with Things effential.

What is the Act of Parliament that terrifies the Confiderer? If he alludes to the Act of Uniformity, his Apprehenfions are groundlefs: Becaufe the propofed *Epinomis* is intended for young Perfons, incapable of *judging* of the Doctrines of the Church:

Whereas

Whereas the *ex animo* Subscription required by the Act of Uniformity, respects *only* such Persons, as are supposed to be capable of *teaching* and *explaining* them. The discerning Author of the *State* does not insinuate that the *Epinomis* should affect those who *do understand* the Articles, but only those who *do not yet* understand them: And thinks, that all popular Objections against this Subscription might be defeated, should it be declared by an explanatory Appendix, that Persons of very tender Years give *all that Assent* to the Articles, which it is *possible* for them to give; and together with that an Engagement for actual Conformity.

By the Constitutions and approved Practice of the Church, *Infants* enter into the Christian Covenant, though incapable of understanding or knowing the Conditions of it.—You will say perhaps, these Infants have their *Sponsors*; and the young *Matriculate* ought to have his. Be it so. If you think the Security insufficient, add, if you please, that of Bondsmen to his personal Obligations. He is of Age to answer, in some Measure at least, for himself. For no Person gains Admission here, who is not arrived at *some Degree of Understanding*; few, that are *unlearned.* Let those, whom it concerns, instruct each Candidate for Matriculation to the *Extent* of his Capacity.

Perhaps

Perhaps it may be found upon Trial, that every such Candidate has Capacity to *learn* as much, as the *proposed Substitute* can *teach*. If he has, he needs no Sponsor; if he has not, let the Sponsor engage to give him the necessary Assistance. If the Candidate finds Difficulties that appear unsurmountable, then let him RETREAT.— Without Controversy, This University, by it's Institution, or rather by it's Constitution, is a Place of Education for *none* but Members of the Church of England. Conformity to the Worship and Articles of the Church is indispensably injoined by her Statutes. This is known to all. Such Persons, as knowing her Conditions approve of them, and will *subscribe* in Testimony of their Approbation, will find a welcome Reception. Persons of a different Persuasion, Persons who cannot with a good Conscience subscribe, may have Recourse to other learned Seminaries, whose Constitution is more conformable to their Tenets and Inclinations.

But why, the Considerer may still ask, should not the Declaration so much spoken of be deemed sufficient, without Subscription? — For many Reasons: Because, for Instance, unwritten Words are transient and unstable: An oral Declaration may be equivocal: It may soon become, alas! Matter of mere Form: Through Inattention,

tention, or through some evil Principle, it may be wholly neglected: It may be made unadvisedly: It may be treated by many as of little Obligation.—On the contrary, *Litera scripta* MANET. Formal Subscription to determinate Propositions precludes *Equivocation*: It is necessarily attended with Ceremonies (the Presence and Monitions of our chief Magistrate, &c.) which preserve it's *Essence*: For the same Reason, it will not be *neglected*; or performed without *Caution*: Though an oral Declaration oftentimes passes for nothing with thoughtless or unprincipled Men; yet a manual Signature is too precise a Testimony of a deliberate Act to be *lightly regarded*: And lastly, WE ought not to acquiesce in an oral Declaration, because a Statute, which we have not a competent Authority to alter, peremptorily requires SUBSCRIPTION.

In our Sister-University we have a laudable and encouraging Example. With a Spirit worthy of their Station, her Rulers have successfully resisted the Faction and Licentiousness of some, and the impertinent "Whispers," or Suggestions of others. And shall this University, the Mirror of Constancy and stedfast Virtue, tremble at the Cry of Alteration, and think of adopting the timid Maxim of "lopping off a Limb to save the Body." The Coward deserves a thousand Deaths, who in a

militant

militant State compounds for Life by the Lofs of a Limb, which ought to be exercifed in the *Defence* of Life. If he adds Perfidy to his Cowardice; if being fworn to obey; and commanded to defend an important Fortrefs, he traiteroufly furrender it; What Difgrace and Punifhment can be equal to his Crimes? The ordinary Iffue is, that fhunning the Danger of an honourable Death, and fhrinking from the Sword of War; he inadvertently encounters with that of Juftice, and dies the Death of a Traitor.

Why fhould we abandon ourfelves to Defpondency? as if our Enemies were mighty, and our Friends unfaithful?— why fhould we not hope for Good from the Mildnefs and Juftice of our governing Superiors, from whom we deferve the beft of Treatment?—But, if this Univerfity muft *now* be the *only* Object of *Perfecution* in the Britifh Dominions: And if " the Cry, which is gone out" againft us muft prevail;—it were better for us to fall by the Hand of another, than by our own.

OXFORD, March 27th, 1772.

D.^r H—l—fx.

No. VI.

Obfervations on two Anonymous Papers, publifhed on March the 21ft and 27th; againft the Confiderations on the Expediency, &c. dated March the 19th, 1772.

THE Author of *the Cafe of Subfcription,* &c. having in his candid Defence joined Iffue in the main Point with the Author of *the Confiderations on the Expediency of making fome Alterations,* &c. a farther Reply on the Subject was deemed unneceffary: but a direct Attack *on the Confiderations,* &c. having appeared Yefterday Evening, it may be proper to fay fomething further in Anfwer to both.

The Author of the Confiderations was not vain enough to imagine, that he could bring over to his own way of thinking, all the Members of Convocation. His fole View in publifhing his Sentiments was, that they might be weighed before the Repeal of the Statute requiring Subfcription at Matriculation came before them in their legiflative Capacity. And he has the Satisfaction to find that a very confiderable Number of the moderate Members of that venerable House concur with him in Opinion: but he is surprized that any of that Body should write with so little Temper as the Author of the last Paper. However, let this be considered as a sufficient Animadversion on that Part of it; which I beg leave to quit for the present.

As the Author of *the Case of Subscription* ingenuously acknowledges that "He "cannot possibly have any Objection to "the projected Mode of *Declaration*, con-"sidered in itself," I begin with the Consequences, which he is apprehensive may ensue from an Alteration.

It is agreed that "the Attack upon our "Subscription took its Rise from that "which was made upon the whole Body "of the Articles:" and it does not appear that certain Members of the House of Commons had any Intention, when the Petition was presented, of proceeding further than the abolishing Subscription at Matriculation. But even supposing they meant to have exempted all *lay* Degrees from what appeared to them an unwarrantable Restraint, what great Inconvenience would arise either to the Universities, or to the Church of *England*, I cannot see; provided a Declaration agreeable to the Acts of Uniformity were made by the Candidates. By this Barrier we should secure their Attendance on the solemn

Services

Services and Rites of Religion, and sufficiently preclude their Oppofition to either the eftablifhed Worfhip or to the Doctrine and Difcipline of the Church. Further than this we ought on no Confideration to go in our Conceffions; and I think no Member of the legiflative Body of this Realm would think of proceeding further, except we fhew a determined Refolution of making no Alteration: in which Cafe, it is impoffible to fay without a prophetic Spirit what may be done. I might mention what I have heard from fome Members of both Houfes of Parliament, and what *they* apprehend would be the Confequence: but it might again be faid that " this " is founding a Retreat before the Face " of the Enemy is feen." I therefore forbear, and beg leave only to add, that when this Point was agitated in the Houfe of Commons, though it appeared that the Church of *England* and the Univerfities had fo many warm Advocates, not one fingle Member of that Body, however well affected to us, could alledge one alleviating Circumftance in our Behalf.

In refpect to the Oath of Supremacy, it is apprehended to be foreign to the prefent Subject. None but Romanifts can object to it; whom it is our Duty to guard againft by all poffible Means: neither have we Power to fufpend the
Ope-

Operation of the Act which obliges many in this Place to take it. Besides that there seems to be an essential Difference between the negative Declaration against the Power of the Pope or any other foreign Prince in these Realms, and a positive Assent to the Truth of a large Collection of abstruse Theological Points. A young Person of 16 or 18 Years of Age may be sufficiently sensible of the Reason of the one, when it is scarcely possible he should be a competent Judge of the other.

I should proceed " to communicate some " of the prudential Reasons, which have " preponderated in the Judgment of those " who are well affected to us," were it not for the Reason just given: but cannot forbear mentioning that I am credibly informed, that when all the Bishops, who were in *London*, (nineteen in Number) met on the 9th Instant, and conferred together on the present Question, they were all unanimous that something effectual ought to be done, and that soon, by each University. They were of Opinion that the best Line that could be drawn was that which the Act of Uniformity prescribed; and saw no Reason for continuing any further Restraint on the other Members of either Body, except that all those who are, or may be, admitted into the

Con-

Convocation or Senate should be obliged to subscribe to the xxxix Articles. As their Lordships therefore cannot be supposed to have been influenced in their Opinions by any other Considerations than the Good of those Seminaries of which they are, or have been, Members, their Proposal will certainly deserve a serious Consideration, if it ever comes before the Universities in Form. It will also I presume be granted, that They have the Interest of the Church of *England* at Heart as much as ourselves; and are as good Judges as we can be of what Concessions the Times require should be made. I have also Authority to add, that our Chancellor and two Representatives are satisfied, that it is incumbent on us to make some Alteration in respect to our present Mode of Subscription; and that his Lordship, who (as I am informed) has already recommended this Matter in a very judicious Letter to the Consideration of his Deputy and Assessors above a Month since, intends to apply soon to Convocation on the same Subject.

I come now to that Paper of the 27th Instant, and here I hope the Author does not expect I should follow him Step by Step. Whatever he may think, I trust the other Members of Convocation will judge it sufficient, if an Answer be given to

the

the few Points which may be thought to have Weight.

If our Author had examined the Charters of the two Univerfities he would not have declared fo peremptorily that "this Uni-"verfity, by it's Inftitution, or rather "Conftitution, is a Place of Education "for *none* but Members of the Church of "*England*." The Charter of *Edward* III. to the Univerfity of *Cambridge*, and the Charter of *Henry* IV. to that of *Oxford*, plainly fhew, that they were confidered in thofe Days (long after their Inftitution) as Seminaries of the liberal Arts, open to all Comers, without Diftinction of Religion or Country. Students from all Parts of *Europe* reforted hither accordingly, till the Reformation naturally reduced their Numbers. The Bounds were fome Time after this ftill more contracted by the Requifition of Subfcription to the Articles in Queen *Elizabeth*'s Time: Since which it is agreed that this Univerfity has been confidered as a Place of Education, for the moft Part, for the Church of *England*; as none but it's Members can enjoy any Emolument, or proceed to Degrees in the Ordinary Way without Subfcriptions: but even now it is not quite fo circumfcribed as our Author afferts. We have had not long fince foreign Gentlemen of different Religions, who have been admitted to ftudy

in

in the Libraries, and have received the Benefit of our public Lectures; and have at this Day some Gentlemen from *Ruſſia* of the *Greek* Religion, whom their Empreſs ſent over to ſtudy in this Place; who, by being admitted to reſide in Colleges or Halls, and living in common with their reſpective Societies, enjoy nearly all the Advantages of *Gremial* Members.

This Author aſſerts poſitively, that "we "have not a competent Authority to alter "the Statute, which peremptorily requires "Subſcription." He will not ſay, however, that we have not ſometimes made Alterations in Statutes, which are of equal Obligation. The Statute relative to Academical Habits, which we new modelled within theſe two Years, is ſurely not forgotten. I might point out ſeveral others, which in the Courſe of theſe laſt twenty Years have been amended or explained: but it is needleſs to dwell longer on *the Fact*. Let us ſee how *the Right*, or "Authority," ſtands. This Point it is confeſſed is not ſo clear at firſt Sight: It may ſtill be remembered what warm Altercations it has produced on ſome former Occaſions. The Arguments then uſed might be here repeated, if it were deemed neceſſary. It was admitted, during the Controverſy, on both Sides, that our municipal Laws (the

H   Statutes,

Statutes, I mean, which we had framed by our sole Authority) might be altered at Pleasure: but it was strongly objected by one of the Parties, that we could under no Pretence whatever meddle with the *Royal Statutes*, without express Authority from the King. Here again another Distinction was made between the Royal Statutes. Some supposed that by these Words were meant all such Statutes, as had been sent down to us from some of our Sovereigns, or at least had been confirmed by them, in Contradistinction to the *Laudian* Code: while others comprehended all those as well as the other under that Denomination, because King *Charles* I. confirmed them all. What was the Consequence? A Case was stated, and laid before Messrs. *Wilbraham* and *Moreton*, who were clearly of Opinion, that we might alter all or any of our Statutes, without Distinction, or Royal Licence. The Alteration proposed was made accordingly: and the last Statute we altered was one of those, which King *Charles* had sent us some Time before he confirmed our present Body of Statutes. The Plea therefore *de Jure* and *de Facto* must be given up; as we cannot pretend to take Shelter under it.

  The Author of the Considerations flatters himself that he is open to Conviction:

viction: but cannot say that he thinks with the Author of the Paper of the 27th that the present Mode of Subscription is so effectual an Exclusion of Papists, or Dissenters, as the proposed Declaration. All that is urged in Favour of the first Mode, holds in his Opinion equally strong in Favour of the latter. The Declaration would be made equally in the Presence of the chief Magistrate, Tutor, &c. so that nothing "would be lost of the "Ceremony, or of any Thing else, which "preserves it's Essence; for which Reason "it would not be neglected, or performed "without Caution." A manual Signature it is thought equally admits of Equivocation as an oral Declaration. And though it be true, that unwritten Words are in their Nature "more transient and unstable" than a Subscription, yet it does not seem to hold in the present Case. For if "by "the Subscription of young Persons no- "thing more be meant, than that they "are Members of the Church of *England*, "and will conform to it's Worship," this End surely will be better answered by an express Declaration to that Effect, than by a forced traditionary Construction, unsupported by any legal Sanction. This Inconvenience has besides been judged to arise from such an Explanation, that young Minds, being so early taught an Instance of *Jesuitism* by their Tutors, will be but too much inclined to extend it to all the other solemn Obligations, which in their maturer Years they may have Occasion to take upon them. Again, I am persuaded that a solemn Declaration will be a better Security than a Subscription in the Manner it is generally managed : for there are many in this Place, who, as I have often heard them say, knew not they had subscribed to the Articles till they saw the Vicechancellor's Certificate. Besides, are not all the public Subscriptions made rather before one of the menial Officers of the University than before the chief Magistrate? Whereas it is hoped that the proposed Declaration would never be made but in his Presence. In a Word, there is great Reason to imagine that within the last ten Years two Papists have been matriculated, who doubtless thought that by the Act of *Matriculation* nothing more was intended than to register their Names with their own Hands among the other Sons of our *Alma Mater :* but the Case might have been different, had they been required to profess themselves Members of the Church of *England* in clear and explicit Terms.

The Example of our Sister University is next proposed for our Imitation : and I confess

confess that every Motion of so respectable a Body in a Case which concerns them *almost* equally with us, deserves our Attention. But what has been done at *Cambridge*? Our Author informs us that "with a Spirit worthy of their Station, her Rulers have successfully resisted the Faction and Licentiousness of some, and the impertinent Whispers," or Suggestions of others: but is not this Information as mere a *gratis dictum*, as any Thing in the Considerations? However, as the Intimations suggested in that Paper have now been fully explained, it is hoped our Author, in Imitation of this Example, will give us a more circumstantial Detail of what the Rulers of that learned Body have done, if he expect we should follow them: otherwise it may be suspected he derives all his Authority from News-papers, than which nothing is in general more fallacious. In the present Case there is the highest Probability, that they have yet come to no Determination. The public Papers (if any Credit is to be given to them) mentioned some Time since, that the Senate had appointed nine of their Members, who, together with the Vicechancellor, were to form a Syndicate to consider of what might be expedient to be done. Whether they have made their Report, and

and what it was; or what Resolution the governing Part of that University have entered upon in Consequence, has not been communicated to the Public through the same Channel, as far as my Information reaches, which I think would scarcely have been omitted, if their Resolution had been formed, as is pretended. I have still a better Reason upon which I ground my Suspicion that this Intelligence is premature; *viz.* that as the chief Magistrate of that Body, as I am credibly informed, acquainted our presiding Magistrate, that their Members had recommended to them to take some Measures to pacify the public Clamours in regard to Subscription, in Consequence of this they were deliberating what Plan should be pursued. Now as a respectful Answer is said to have been sent from hence, and no Answer yet received, I must beg Leave still to suspend my Belief as to this Article.

Our Author concludes his Paper with an Exhortation to Firmness, in a Style truly rhetorical and pathetic. But the University is not to be influenced by mere Declamation. Words directed to rouze the Passions of grave and learned Men lose their Effect; while Reasons proposed to their Understanding may have Weight.

Upon

Upon the Whole, I hope our brave Champion will reserve his Courage for some fitter Occasion; and, though he seems to detest an Act of Suicide, I flatter myself he will have no Opportunity given him of becoming a Martyr.

OXFORD, March 28th, 1772.

Dr D——c

No. VII.

No. VII.

Further Considerations upon the Expediency of making some Alteration in regard to Subscription in the XXXIX Articles in this University.

THE Author of the *Considerations*, &c. has already delivered both his own Sentiments upon the Subject, as drawn from *prudential* Motives, and the Sentiments of some others, as drawn from the *Reason* of the Thing. How far they *have* Reason on their Side, He does not say.

The following Reflections may come in aid of what has been already advanced on this side of the Question, which seems divisible into two Heads, the *Propriety* of making Alterations, and the *Right* to alter. I begin with the former.

My first Argument against Subscription at Matriculation shall be taken from the unsatisfactory Reasons, hitherto urged, in behalf of the Practice.

1. The Case of young Persons, of no more than twelve Years of Age, subscribing to the Articles, has been stated as nearly parallel to that of young Men of sixteen or eighteen abjuring the Pope's Supremacy, which Abjuration is at that Age required.

required. But need I point out the wide Difference between the two Cases, in a double Respect? I mean the *Age* of the Abjurers, and the *Point* which they abjure. The former subscribes to a Variety of Propositions of profound Argument, and of a mixed Nature, Historical, Theological, and Metaphysical; the latter yield their Assent to one simple Proposition, and declare that they will allow the Pope no Right in the Ecclesiastical and Spiritual Concerns of these Kingdoms. The former have confessedly, and by general Consent, not yet attained to Years of Judgment and Discretion; the latter have not only attained, but exceeded, that Age.

2. The Advocates of such Subscription not only acknowledge that it amounts to no more than a mere Declaration of Conformity to the Doctrine and Discipline of the Church of *England*, but, moreover, that by this Explanation they *put the best Face upon the Matter* they can devise. If this be the best Face you can put upon the Matter, says the Adversary to such Subscription, and no Assent to the Articles from the Party subscribing be either expected or required, there is something very aukward and ugly in this Face; it is not so much a Face, as a Mask; and, like many other Masks, it's leading Feature is monstrous and distorted. If it is Subscription without

out Assent to the Propositions, it is no Subscription to the Articles at all: if it is a Subscription to the Articles as a Test only of Conformity to the Liturgy, it is then Subscription to one of the Articles of the Thirty-sixth Canon, but not to the Thirty-nine Articles. In either Case, the Conveniences of such Subscription are overbalanced by the Inconveniences. The only Convenience I can perceive is, the probable Security, that the Person so subscribing will, by such a previous Act, be induced to examine the Articles with Attention, and by a Kind of Prepossession be led to adopt their real Sense, when called upon in Form.——— The Inconveniences are,

1st, The probable Imputation of Chicanery and double Dealing implied in the Notion, that the Party, though subscribing to the Articles as a Test, yet does not consider them as a Test in the same Light in which they are considered by the Law of the Land.

2dly, The Mischief that may arise from introducing a Laxness of Principle, in his subsequent Subscriptions. For if Subscription to Articles, without acknowledging the Truth of the Propositions contained in them, be formally admitted at Matriculation, the same Latitude of Construction may be transferred by him to the taking of Degrees. If Subscription may be bent to
such

such an Interpretation in Cases where we have no Exception, it may be adopted in Cases where we allow it to be highly exceptionable.

3dly, Subscription so interpreted is arbitrary and unauthorized. It never had any express and avowed Sanction of Weight, because it never *could* have any: *all* Subscription to the Articles being equally, in the Intention of those who enjoined it, sincere and *ex animo*. Subscription, in any other Construction, is not the Subscription *required*. And they who contend for it in any other Sense, contend for a Shadow.

4thly, It is capricious and inconsistent; as it may happen to be at Variance with its own Principle, by dispensing with Assent to the Propositions in some Persons, and requiring it from others of inferior Age to those in whom it is dispensed with. For some are older at Matriculation, than others are at the taking of Degrees. Supposing therefore your *Epinomis* both legal and justifiable, yet it cannot with Propriety operate at Matriculation universally and indiscriminately; the dispensing with Assent will, upon your own Hypothesis, be as unreasonable in the one Case, as requiring it in the other.

I ask then, Is Subscription to the Thirty-nine Articles the *only* Test that I am a Friend to the Church of *England?* If it is; such a Test, as being necessary, must be required of *all*, in its full and proper Sense: if it is not the only Test; why impose it on any of those, from whom you acknowledge a Declaration of Conformity to the Liturgy to be a sufficient Security.

A full Persuasion of the Sufficiency of such a Declaration is, as I conceive, the Motive which has induced many grave and sensible Persons to wish that none were obliged, in our Universities, to subscribe to the Thirty-nine Articles, excepting such as are included in the Act of Uniformity, together with those who commence Members of the Convocation at *Oxford* and of the Senate at *Cambridge*. These, as being more immediately intrusted either with the Regimen of particular Societies, or with the Legislation of the University, and being generally of riper Years, are supposed to have formed their Principles, and to subscribe upon full Judgment and Conviction: on which Account their Subscription being more sincere, their Attachment to it will be the more permanent. And indeed, to speak my Mind, How either the Church or the Universities are likely to tumble into Ruins, merely on Account of the postponing of Subscription to the Articles till Graduates commence Regents, (allowing the Act of Uniformity in the mean Time it's full Force) I cannot conceive.

Supposing

Suppofing then, for the prefent, that fuch Alteration is highly *reafonable*, as well as expedient, the next point is, Has this Univerfity *Power and Authority* to make fuch Alteration?

The Argument alledged to prove that we have no fuch Power, is, that the Statute requiring Subfcription in it's prefent Mode, though made by the Univerfity alone at the Inftance of Lord *Leicefter*, yet having been afterwards adopted in the Body of Statutes compiled by Arch-Bifhop *Laud*, was enforced by the joint Authority of the Sovereign and the Univerfity: And that this, and fuch like Statutes, we have alfo taken an Oath not to alter, explain, or abrogate without Royal Licence.

I anfwer, Firft, that, upon the fame Principle of reafoning, it is not in our Power to make an *Epinomis*; fuch *Epinomis* being an *Explanation* of the Statute, and confequently an Infringement of the Sovereign's Right. And I believe neither the *Manes* of *Leicefter* nor of *Laud* will thank the Authors of fuch a Propofal.

Secondly, I do not fcruple to pronounce that the Authority of the Sovereign in this Matter was *ab Origine* null and void: the Sovereign at that Time having been never poffeffed of any more Right to interfere with the making or enforcing of the Statutes of this Univerfity-Corporation, than his

his present Majesty has to make Laws for the Mayor and Corporation of *Oxford*. And this Doctrine will be found upon Enquiry, to be consistent not only with the Opinion of Common Lawyers, consulted heretofore upon similar Occasions; but also with our own Practice. We *have* already altered and explained such Royal Statutes. But whether we had, or had not, altered and explained them of ourselves, we have always had the Right so to do, inherent in us as a Body Corporate, and have the same Right still. And what would those Gentlemen, who upon the present Occasion thus compliment away our essential Privileges, say, were any Person to make the Experiment in these Times; and, upon the Strength of such an imaginary Precedent, attempt to introduce anew such an illegal and arbitrary Power, by advising or permitting his Majesty King GEORGE the Third to give his *joint Authority* to a new-made Statute? I ween He would deem it Perfidy and Cowardice itself, and would pronounce, that the Traitor who encouraged such an Encroachment upon our Rights, *deserved to die a thousand Deaths*. But if such a Proceeding would be unconstitutional *now*, it was unconstitutional *then*. The Act of ELIZ. 13. was as much in Force in those Days, as in the present; and the indiscreet Conduct of our Predecessors in
conceding

conceding a temporary Right to the Sovereign, which Right was, by the Act abovementioned, exclusively vested in this University as a. Body Corporate, can never in Law amount to a Forfeiture of our Privileges, however powerfully it may operate in the Construction or Disposition of some of our own Members. But if there be any who think this Royal Authority of the least Weight, let them in their Consciences act accordingly. I only desire leave to think, that whatever Weight it had then, it died with the Sovereign who gave it, and can never bind by Proxy. But, as I have already observed, it's binding Force *was* and *is* a Non-entity.

With Respect to " consulting our Chancellor" upon this Business, it is both decent and proper; and I doubt not our Governors in this Place will treat their first Magistrate with due Respect. At the same Time I cannot allow, that what has been ordained at the Instance of one Chancellor, must never be cancelled but by the *Judgment and Approbation* of another; as such Doctrine might, in other Times, (as probably it has in some) tend to establish and perpetuate not only an unnecessary, but a despotic, Power, in a free, and (as I hope it will always continue) an independent Corporation.

OXFORD, March 28, 1772.

No. VIII.

THE Author of a Paper dated March 27th is not fond of *Egotism*: But as the Titles of Writers upon our Subscription are become pretty numerous, he finds it troublesome to repeat them; and therefore will sometimes as his Antagonist does always speak in the first Person singular.

I had never seen or heard of the "Defence" written by the Author of the *Case stated* till I read the "Observations." The Observer is artful enough in giving to that Paper the flattering Denomination of a "Candid DEFENCE." Whether it does or does not deserve that Title, it makes no Alteration in my Sentiments with respect to the *Subject*, but only with respect to the *Author*: There indeed I am sensibly affected; and observe with much Concern such a Mixture of *Clay* in a Figure, which I thought wholly to consist of *standard Gold*. If however I, who am "*our* Author's brave Champion," must needs become a Principal; when I expected to be a Second; I will still keep up my Spirits; and I have Confidence that "my Courage" will never fail me. I shall made the best Use I can of my *Sling* and my *Scrip*, with which I shall boldly advance into the Front of the Battle: Though I am apprehensive that my Contest must be, not with one GOLIAH only;

only; but with a little Army of Philiftines. For, to drop the Allufion, I am of Opinion, that the *Obfervations* are not the Work of a *fingle* Hand; or evidently, not of the *fame* Hand, which produced the *Confiderations*. I rejoice and glory in the Succefs of my paft Labours: They have vifibly been very ufeful already in one Inftance, in compelling the *Obferver* to be rather more explicit than the *Confiderer* had been, and to convert his former *gratis Dicta* and Whifpers into fomething more authentick. As he feems to be in the Cabinet, it would have been commendable in him to have been ftill more open to the Members of Convocation, who are to be Judges in the Difpute; and to have communicated to them " fome of thofe prudential Reafons, which preponderate in the Judgement" of the great and wife: For *Reafons* are the things which juftly claim our Regard; while mere *Intimations* from anonymous Writers have as little Influence with Men of Senfe and Learning, as " *mere Declamation*."

When the Author of *Obfervations* " came to *that* (*l.* that there) Paper of the 27th Inftant," it might reafonably have been expected from him to attend to a *few* more *Points* than he has done. He ought to have fhown the Mifapplication or Fallacy of thofe Topics, which were propofed in Oppofition

position to his own Reasonings; and should have invalidated the Arguments, urged in Defence or Explanation of the *Case stated.* I have the Satisfaction to find that they are much approved of by Men of Judgement and Integrity: And do not yet take it for granted, that (in the Author's polite Language) "the other Members of Convocation" will be so easily satisfied with *Hints* from the Cabinet, as our Author of Observations "flatters himself" that they will.

1. I asserted, that " without Controversy this University, by it's Constitution, is a Place of Education for none but Members of the Church established." It was said, " *without Controversy,*" because the Writers who had gone before me, on each Side of the Question (namely, the Author of the *State,* and the Author of *Considerations)* instead of *controverting,* had allowed it: I changed Institution to Constitution; because I was willing to *correct* an Error in one of the Parties, without openly *remarking* it: I now maintain that, by it's present Constitution, it is a Place of Education for *none* but Members of the Church of England: Because the Advantages politely allowed to Foreigners in some Colleges and Halls, are merely private *Indulgences* unauthorized and unnoticed by our publick Statutes: And those Foreigners (who might be of the *Romish* as well as of the
Greek

Greek Church) are neither *Members* of thoſe private Societies, nor of the Univerſity. Thus an unnaturalized Portugueſe Jew is allowed to *live* in *England*, and to " enjoy many of the Advantages" of our Civil Conſtitution.——What then?—Is that Conſtitution calculated or deſigned for *his* Emolument? or, will the Obſerver aſſert, that he dwells *in aliena Republica*, as in a Place intended for univerſal Traffic, " where " all Comers, without Diſtinction," are received and treated as natural or free-born Subjects?

2. It would be irkſome to *revive* at this Time Diſputes concerning the Authority of the Univerſity to alter their Statutes. But it is proper to obſerve, that the current and prevailing Opinion has always been, that *Royal* Statutes could not be altered without *Royal* Licence. Such Vouchers for the Truth of this Aſſertion might be produced, as it is believed the Author of the Obſervations would not chooſe to gainſay. The Inſtances of recent Acts of Convocation, " which ſeem at firſt Sight" to contradict this Aſſertion, are in Reality altogether conſiſtent with it. Many of us well remember, that when the *Reſponſes* of Mr. *Wilbraham* and Mr. *Moreton* were firſt made known to the Univerſity, ſome Perſons of great Reputation conſidered them as frivolous, or inconſiſtent: Others thought them

them indefinite, unsatisfactory, and unintelligible: And some were even convinced by them of the Truth of the *opposite Opinion*. Although a great Majority of the University assented to the *qualifying* Explanation recommended by Mr. *Wilbraham* and Mr. *Moreton:* Yet that was done by many upon a much better Principle than the *Authority* of the learned Gentlemen of the Law. It was considered, that the "*Simul non fruendis*" was reconcileable to the *Restoration* of a *quondam Member:* And the proper Steps being previously taken, that *Re-Instation* was assented to by a great Majority. Some Gentlemen, however, of very respectable Character would *not* assent to it; who are at this Time Members of this University; and it is believed, well-known to and regarded by the Author or Authors of " Observations." It would be fruitless to dwell longer upon this Subject: bring the Matter therefore to a short Issue. —The Statutes of the University forbid the Alteration of a royal Statute, by the sole Authority of the University. The Statute requiring Subscription to Articles is a royal Statute. *Ergo*, &c. It is hoped that the Observer will think *this* one of the *few Points* which may be worthy of a further Answer.

3. Though the Author of Considerations thinks, that a " manual Signature equally admits

admits of Equivocation as an oral Declaration" does: Yet it is believed by his Antagonift, "that the other Members of Con-" vocation will think" differently. I need not repeat what has been faid upon that Point in the Paper of the 27th Inftant: but I earneftly recommend it to the ferious Confideration of every impartial Reader. There is another Part of that Paper which the Obferver " fteps" over, and either through Pride or Fear, will not vouchfafe or venture to fet his Foot upon. This is a Vindication of the Statutes of the Univerfity in requiring the Subfcription of young Perfons—from the approved Practice of the Church in admitting *Infants* into the chriftian Covenant. Let the Obferver know, that the impartial Publick will not be fatisfied with a ———" whatever *he* may " think," applied to an Opponent: THEY will, no doubt, think as I do, that when the Obferver refufes to follow his Antagonift " Step by Step," and profeffes to give an Anfwer to a "*few Points*" only; the Reafon why he does not anfwer *other* Points is fuch as he is afhamed to own, It is a pretty kind of Contemplation to the Writer, I fuppofe, to feem to bounce and vapour with a few contemptuous and common-place Sarcafms, of " *he* may think," and " I truft," and " mere Declamation," and " little Temper," &c. I envy him

not

not that Amusement in *private: Sua se jactet in* AULA, after this Manner as much as he pleases: But Attention to *every Argument* is expected by the Publick from one, who would be thought to exhibit his Opinions, for the Sake of conveying or receiving Conviction.

4. In the Paper of the 27th an effectual Method was recommended for preventing mental Reservation and *Jesuitical* Equivocation. But this also the Observer thinks of *so* little Weight, as boldly to " step" over it unnoticed.—If there be any Tutors amongst us, who in any Instance whatever teach " *Jesuitism*" to their Pupils, this would be a *new* Argument in favour of Subscription. For I must still insist upon it, (though my Opponent *thinks* otherwise) that a manual Signature is a better Security against *Jesuitical* Equivocation, than an oral Declaration can be. If again, " many Persons have subscribed to the Articles without knowing it;" this is indeed a Mark of very criminal Negligence in the Tutor and others: But the Inference from hence against Subscription would be equally applicable to an oral Declaration. If the Subscription is ever made " rather before a menial Servant * than the chief Magistrate

---

* Whom does the Author mean by a menial Servant? Can he give that Appellation to a 'Squire-Bedel?---or does he mean the domestic Servant of the Vice-Chancellor? In either Case however, our chief Magistrate OUGHT to preside.

trate of the University"———let the Blame fall where the Offence is—These Things OUGHT not so to be—And there is equal Reason to hope that Subscription, no less than the proposed Declaration, might for the future be made in HIS Presence. If the NEWS be true, that " two Papists have been *matriculated* within these ten Years," this is indeed exceeding alarming: It ought to excite publick Enquiry into the Principles of the TUTOR, by whom they were recommended: It ought to put us all upon our Guard against *Jesuits* in DISGUISE. The dark Counsels, which now appear to have been a long Time fostering in the Breast of the Observer and his " moderate" Friends, may justly raise Suspicion. Our History affords us Warnings and Examples.—Who the Observer is, I know not; nor do I with Certainty know, who are his *Coadjutors:* But as he often speaks with *Authority*, we have the greatest Reason to fear.

5. Yes, indeed; I freely acknowledge that my Intelligence concerning our Sister University is " derived from News-Papers." I never had the Honour of conversing or corresponding upon the Subject of Subscription either with the chief Magistrate of that learned Seminary, or with any of the Members of either House of Parliament. The News-Papers are (I must confess) oftentimes

" falla-

"fallacious." And yet when an Article of Intelligence, relating to a *Fact* of *Notoriety* and *Importance*, is communicated to the Publick and never contradicted; there seems to be no great Reason to question it's Authenticity. My Opponent may perhaps be in the Secrets of that University, as well as in the *Cabinet* of this. He probably knows a great deal more concerning their Proceedings than I do. But I believe the following Particulars are such as he cannot contradict: That much Resistance has been made against " the Spirit of Faction" there; that the Assailants have hitherto been in such a Manner withstood, as to have gained no Ground; and that the *Grace of Thanks* for the Interposition of their Representatives, was *refused*. The " Syndicate" I never heard of, till I read the " Observations."

There cannot be " a fitter Occasion for a brave Champion's Courage" than the present. The Cause is that of the Church of England, and of this University one of it's firmest Pillars.——Though I would not " flatter myself" so much, as my Opponent does, yet in Compliment to his Sincerity, I accept, with Thanks and Pride, the honourable Mention he has made of me, in the last Paragraph of " Observations;" and I assure him in Return, that, if I have any Taste or Discernment in literary Compofitions, *that Part* of the Paper is *truely* ORATORICAL. The Obferver *there* becomes of a fudden brifk and facetious; and it were a Pity to be fo grave as not to allow it's Effect to his *only* Joke: I therefore *fmile* when I fpeak of it. And yet it's Abfurdity and Ill-nature quickly check my good Humour, when I obferve that inftead of wifhing me to *live* and *not die*, He " flatters himfelf," that I fhall die by an " Act of Suicide," which he fays I " feem to deteft;" and even envies me the Confolation of an honourable Martyrdom. I would not be fo much wanting in Chriftian Charity, as not to return Good for Evil; and therefore, though I think a Sacrifice of any *public* Good or Security too great an *Atonement* for the Offence of an *Individual*, yet I affure him with the utmoft Sincerity that I no more *wifh* him to come to any untimely End, than I *expect* him to die a Martyr.

OXFORD, March 31, 1772.

D?. *Sc—l—f—*

No. IX.

THE Author of *the Case, &c.* would not have presumed to have troubled his Readers with any Thing more about the Subscription, had he not thought the Credit and Honour of the University particularly concerned in having right Notions ascertained as to the Meaning and Intention of the present Mode of Subscription. The Writer of the *Considerations* having over and over again insisted upon an indefensible State of the Case, he thought himself under a Necessity of appearing in Print once more, and for the last Time.

He has expressly charged the Governors of the University, for near two Hundred Years past, down to this very Day, with having required from young Persons, at their Matriculation, a *formal Assent to the Truth of a Variety of Propositions of profound Argument, and of a mixed Nature, Historical, Theological, and Metaphysical*, which they knew it was impossible for them to understand. And yet he is so indulgent as to wish, *that this Practice might have continued without Impeachment for many hundred Years more*. Now on the contrary,

contrary, I do aver, that if this had been their Intention, they have all along been the moſt unreaſonable, abſurd, and iniquitous Set of Governors that ever lived; and the Practice ought not to have obtained for a ſingle Day.

After this Preamble, may I be permitted to make a few very ſhort Strictures upon ſome Paragraphs of the laſt Paper, as they are marked in it, 1, 2, &c.

I. Does the Oath of Supremacy intend nothing more than a bare Denial of the Pope's Authority? Do not the Words, " No *foreign* Prince, Prelate, &c." import an Acknowledgment of the King's Supreme Authority in all Matters *Eccleſiaſtical and Spiritual?* Nay, does not the very *Statute of Matriculation* call it an Oath *De agnoſcendo Primatu Regiæ Majeſtatis?*

II. The invidious Turn given to the Author's Expreſſion in the Witticiſm of the Maſk does not deſerve his Regard. He is not aſhamed to wear the ſame Face, and to ſhew it too, as the beſt and greateſt Men of this Univerſity have long worn. Again.

I. There is no Chicanery in making a Subſcription, according to the Intention of the Impoſers. Whether the *Author of the Caſe*, or the *Conſiderer*, has rightly repreſented that Intention, is left to the Judgment

Judgment of others.—I know no Law of the Land which interferes in this Matter.—I know that all Laws are to be interpreted according to the Intention of their Makers.

II. The Account lately publiſhed of the Origin of the Subſcription, might have ſaved the *Conſiderer* this Paragraph. Tutors are directed, even by the Statute itſelf, *Tit.* 3. 2. to be very careful to inſtruct their Pupils in the Senſe of the Articles, before they take their Degrees. This ſhews they were not ſuppoſed to have been ſufficiently, if at all, inſtructed in them, when they came to the Univerſity. And there is a very obſervable Difference in the Form of Subſcription. The Candidate for a Degree, declares ſolemnly, and ſubſcribes to the Declaration, that after having read the Thirty-nine Articles, he finds them *to be all agreeable to the Word of God.* The young Perſon matriculated ſigns his Name in a Book to which the Articles are prefixed, without being required to have read them; nor is he required to give any *formal Aſſent* to the Truth of the Doctrines contained in them. If ſuch *Aſſent* was intended, why is he not likewiſe required to give it *?

---

* What is mentioned in this Paragraph will ſhortly be more fully explained, and in a Manner that will leave no Room for a Reply.

III. Every Tutor may, I think, satisfy himself, and he ought, in Duty, always to satisfy his Pupils of the real Intention and Meaning of the Subscription. If any Sanction of Public Authority is necessary, let it have one. The Oath which young Persons are obliged to take at their Matriculation, to observe the Statutes, was as much cried out against as the present Subscription. The *Epinomis* gave Satisfaction in the former Case; why may not another of the like Kind do the same in the latter?

IV. The Difference of Age from *twelve* to *sixteen*, is not so much to be regarded, as the Improvements the young People are supposed to make in the Course of four Years Study. One who takes his Batchelor's Degree at the Age of *sixteen*, is presumed to have as much Knowledge in all the Sciences, wherein he is required to be instructed, as one who is matriculated at *sixteen*, and takes his Degree at the Age of *twenty*.

The Author of *the Case, &c.* has offered his Plea in behalf of the Practice of the University. If it is a right one, they stand acquitted of all untoward Imputations. But if the *Considerer*'s Explanation be admitted, and the Governors of the University have *blindly* continued for a
long

long Series of Years in an unwarrantable, abſurd, and irreligious Practice; they not only ought to abrogate it immediately, but to write a Letter of Thanks to Sir W. M. for having opened their Eyes.

Dr. I—t—p—

No. X.

A Vindication of the Test at Matriculation, in it's present Mode, from the plausible Objections that have been raised against it.

IT hath been artfully thrown out by the avowed Enemies of the Church of *England* as now established, that the Subscription to it's Articles required by this University at Matriculation is a scandalous and unjustifiable Imposition on mere Boys, who cannot in Reason be supposed qualified to judge of the Sense of them.——Many steady Friends to the Church and University have been startled at the Plea; and thinking it a Practice altogether indefensible, are therefore, in the true and candid Spirit of the Church of *England*, zealous for the Alteration of it.——But before we allow the Charge, let us see whether it doth not rest on a mere Mistake.——The Wisdom of Ages ought not in Justice to give Way suddenly to every seeming Difficulty.

All the Arguments hitherto urged in Favor of an Alteration of the present Mode of Test at Matriculation, depend on a Supposition, that by this Subscription the University requires an actual positive Assent to the Truth of the Doctrines contained in the xxxix Articles.

If this were really the Case, the Objections are unanswerable, and a Test of another Kind ought to be substituted in it's room.——But if it appear that no such Assent either is, or ever was intended to be required by the University, then the present Mode is not affected by any Arguments yet urged against it.

I presume it will be universally granted, that in whatever Sense the University requires this Subscription, in that Sense, and no other, the Subscription is made.

From the Manner of Proceeding at the Admission of a Scholar we may fairly collect in what Sense the University actually does, and always did, consider it.——The Scholar before he is admitted is required to subscribe the xxxix Articles, but simply, without any Formula expressive of *Assent* to the Truth of the Doctrines contained in them.——He is not even required to have read them.——And his Tutor is enjoined by Statute to instruct him in the Sense of them, Tit. III. §. 2. " *Tutor verò Scho-*
" *lares Tutelæ & Regimini suo commissos pro-*
" *bis Moribus imbuat, & in probatis Au-*
" *thoribus instituat; & maximè in Rudimen-*
" *tis Religionis & Doctrinæ Articulis in Sy-*
" *nodo Lond. (anno* 1562) *editis: ac pro*
" *virili suo Disciplinæ in Ecclesiâ Anglicanâ*
" *publicè receptæ eos conformes præstabit.*"

This

This last Circumstance proves to a Demonstration that the University does not suppose the Scholar already fully informed in the meaning of the Articles, and therefore cannot (without a Contradiction too gross to be suspected in an Institution with any Pretensions to Wisdom) be supposed to require a full and entire Assent to what it owns it does not imagine him to comprehend.

And if this Subscription does not imply an entire Assent to the Truth of every Proposition contained in the Articles, it can necessarily imply no Assent at all. For to say that it is an Assent as far as the Scholar understands them, is to make it no Test, unless an Acquiescence in the rest which he does not understand be also implied. And if an Acquiescence be allowed sufficient for a Part, it is equally so for the Whole. There is therefore no Medium; this Subscription must either mean an entire Assent, or merely an Acquiescence. That it cannot mean an entire Assent is already proved; an *Acquiescence* then is all that is, or ever was intended.

It may be asked, what Right the University has to understand Subscription, in this Instance, in a different Sense from what it is allowed by general Consent, and by the University itself, to have in every other Instance. Is not this a dangerous Doctrine,

Doctrine, full of Chicane and double dealing, and subversive of all Subscription to any good Purpose?——By those who ask these Questions it is taken for granted that a bare Subscription, of Necessity can imply no less than an entire Assent to what is so subscribed.——Now this is certainly not true in all Cases.——I might instance in Affairs of common Negociation in civil Matters. But it will be sufficient to the present Purpose to show that there is no Instance in which the xxxix Articles are subscribed where an Assent is intended to be required, but what that Assent is expressed in Terms, and not supposed to follow from the mere Subscription.

How is it in the University?——When the Matriculated Scholar becomes a Candidate for a Degree, he is again required to subscribe the 39 Articles; and moreover the three Articles of the 36th Canon, which include an Allowance of the xxxix Articles, and an Acknowledgment that they are agreeable to the Word of God.

And this Subscription was * originally made, not simply, but in the following
‘ Form :

---

* This Formula was decreed by Convocation in the Year 1616, but not incorporated into the present Body of Statutes. And indeed it would be superfluous, as the three Articles of the 36th Canon are in a declaratory Form, and amount to the same Thing. These Articles are not only subscribed, but actually read by the Candidate, at the Time of his Presentation.

Form:——" *Ego A. perlectis prius vel ab*
" *alio coràm me recitatis Orthodoxæ Fidei &*
" *Religionis Articulis xxxix in sacrâ Synodo*
" *Lond. habitâ A. D.* 1562 *constabilitis*;
" *simulque tribus Capitibus in aliâ Synodo*
" *Londinensi sub Annum* 1604 *decretis &*
" *in Canone* 36*to redactis sciens volensque ex*
" *animo subscribo.*" And the Person who presents is also required to attest that the Candidate hath read, or heard read, the Articles to which he hath subscribed.—— In this Case the University certainly intends to require a full and entire Assent; and has a good Right to do it, having before provided proper Means of Instruction. The Assent is clearly expressed; and all possible Caution taken that it may not be given in a thoughtless and precipitate Manner.

How is it in Subscriptions not merely Academical?—No Man ought to be admitted either to the Order of Deacon or Priest, unless he first subscribe to the xxxix Articles. Stat. 13 Eliz. c. 12.—This simple Subscription is all that is required for Deacons Orders; and need imply no more than a mere Acquiescence. But if a Deacon take upon him, or be licensed, *to preach*, he can maintain nothing contrary to the Doctrine of the xxxix Articles, on Pain of Deprivation, unless he recant. Stat. 13 Eliz. c. 12.

But the Case is different with Respect to a Priest, of whom positive Profession is required.

"*No Bishop ought to make any Deacon a Priest, unless he first bring to the Bishop, from Men known to the Bishop to be of sound Religion, a Testimonial both of his honest Life and of his* PROFESSING *the Doctrine expressed in the Articles of Religion agreed upon by a National Synod in the Year* 1562." Stat. 13 Eliz. c. 12.

At Institution to a Benefice with Cure of Souls, the instituted Person ought to subscribe the Articles before the Ordinary by his own voluntary Act; and when he takes Possession of his Benefice, he is obliged by Law to read the Articles in the Church, and declare his *unfeigned Assent* to them.

Hence I conclude, that whenever an *Assent* to the Articles is intended to be required, it is always expressed.

It is also evident from what has been said, that by the simple Subscription of Matriculation the University can understand nothing but a mere Acquiescence.

An Acquiescence is the least Security the University as a Seminary for the Church of *England* can possibly require; and such a Test cannot be a Burthen' to the Conscience of any who take it; and can exclude none but such as it is the Duty of the University to exclude.

It

It is further evident, that by so understanding it the University does not adopt a singular or unwarranted Notion of Subscription, or by any Means countenance the Subscribing in various lax and indeterminate Senses, where an Assent is required.

OXFORD, April 3, 1772.

Dr. B—gh

No. XI.

No. XI.

OUR Disputes are now come to a *Crisis*. The learned Author of the *State*, and his ingenious Friend the *Vindicator* are so decisive upon the *Propriety* and *Expediency* of the present Mode of Subscription, as to leave no Room for Cavil or Objection. There seems also to be very little Reason for the Friends of Novelty to insist any longer upon that other controverted Subject, the Authority of the University to alter an original Statute. But as the Writer of " Further " Observations" may perhaps expect that some Notice should be taken of what he has advanced in Support of that Authority, I shall offer a Word or two in Reply to him, and then bid a final Adieu to the Controversy.

1. To the Author's first *Answer* I reply; that the *Epinomis*, if it should be thought expedient to make one, would no more be an Infringement of the *Sovereign*'s *Right*, than the Annotations of a *Commentator* are an Infringement of the Sense of the *Author*. The Interpretation, put upon the Statute by learned Men, might be a *Guide* to Persons less learned, but no Obligation upon their Consciences, inconsistent with their

their own Convictions of the *Sense* of the Statute.

To the second Answer, I reply thus.—The KING of England NEVER *dies*; therefore his Acts cannot die "WITH him". The Charters and Grants for Instance of King George the first, if not limited to Time, are as valid in the Year 1772, as they were in 1721.——But this is not all. The Confirmation of Charles the first was *expresly* made perpetual; *Pro Nobis et Heredibus et Successoribus Nostris*.—If the Sanction died with the Sovereign; those Members of the University, who *on the Day appointed* bound themselves by Oath to maintain the *New Code* were released from the Obligation of that Oath either in Whole or in Part on the thirtieth of January 1649. And yet we never hear of their *renewing* their Obligation to the Laws of the University in general; or, of their thinking themselves *exempt* from any *Part* of their Obligation.—If their Obligation was *temporary*, the *Limitation* of Time must by the Maxims of Law and Reason have been *expressed*: The Author would do well to find out the *Record* of such a Limitation. —The *Interference* of the Sovereign was not by an arbitrary Injunction, but by an Act of *Favour*. Should " his present Ma-" jesty" at the Request of the " Mayor, " &c. of *Oxford*," grant them a new Charter

Charter for the *better Government* of their Town and Corporation: They would "*I ween*" find themselves confined by certain *Provisos*; and the *Bye-Laws*, which they might occasionally enact, would be *null and void*, if repugnant to *their Charter* ——They might *personally* incur the Guilt and Penalties of *Perjury*; and in their political Capacity forfeit their Charter by *Misuser*.—— The "Conduct of Predecessors" however "*indiscreet*" would be as *obligatory* upon Successors as their own Act would.

2. The Author of the Paper dated March the 27. never would think of "ad- "*vising* his Majesty to give Authority for "the making of a *new Statute*;" but he knows his Majesty's Consent to be necessary for the altering of *some old ones*.

3. If this University has ever *done*, what it had no *Right* to do, the *Act* itself is invalid, and the *Example* is of no Authority. The Author of Observations is extremely apt to argue from *bad Examples*; and against the Existence of good Rules from the *Neglect* of them.

Amongst many other Instances of *Self-Flattery* the Author seems to "flatter him- "self" by too high an Opinion of the Number of his Friends. I have great Reason to believe that a considerable Majority of those venerable Personages who in Wis-
-dom

dom and Authority ſtand firſt in our Academical Legiſlature, are averſe to the propoſed Innovation. One of them in particular, who had been ſuſpected of giving too much Countenance to our Enterprizers in Reformation, aſſures me that his Inclination and Opinion upon this Subject are entirely conformable to my own. The Severity which he has lately experienced *from ſome of his Superiors,* and which every candid Perſon muſt condemn, induces him to be ſilent and cautious, but not to forget his Duty. This Conduct is prudent and truly commendable: And I believe his Profeſſions to be perfectly ſincere. I am alſo credibly informed, that if ever the Zeal of many of his Brethren is brought to the Trial, it will diſcover itſelf in an inſuperable Affection to the Church eſtabliſhed, and a great Regard to our preſent Academical Polity. May ſuch Sentiments prevail.

OXFORD, April 4, 1772.   *D.ʳ H—l-f—*

No. XII.

No. XII.

THE Affair of the Subscription has been much agitated. I have considered what has been said on all Sides; and I hope it will not be thought impertinent, if I state the Case according to my Notions of the Debate, without presuming to direct the Judgment of others.

The following Positions strongly oppose any projected Alteration.

The University has a *prescriptive Right* to the present Mode of Subscription, having exercised it for near two Hundred Years.

It cannot be presumed, that so learned a Body would have instituted and continued a Practice, *unwarrantable, arbitrary, and absurd.*

The only Construction that can make it otherwise is, that they had no farther Intention in requiring a Subscription to the Articles from young Persons at their Matriculation, than that they should declare their *Acquiescence* in the Doctrines of the Church of England, which all the Members of it, of whatever Degree, who do not give *any formal or explicit Assent* to them, are supposed to *acquiesce* in.

This

This their *Intention* has been made to appear so fully, that there cannot remain any reasonable Doubt about it.

There have been no evil Suspicions, no Uneasiness in this Place, arising from the Continuance of the Practice. It has generally been looked upon as a proper Method to secure the Interests of the Church of England, which the Nature of our Constitution requires us to guard.

Any Alteration of the Practice might seem to carry in it a Reflection upon the Wisdom and Piety of our Predecessors, for having *established* it, and an Acknowledgment of the Want of them in ourselves, for having *continued* it.

It may be apprehended, that such a supposed Acknowledgment may operate so as to affect very materially the Articles of our Church, there being too much Reason to think, that the Outcry against the University Subscription arises more from a Dislike to the Articles themselves, than from a tender Concern for the Consciences of our Youth.

If the Subscription is defensible upon Principles that want only to be made known to gain the Approbation of all reasonable and true Members of our Church, why should we not maintain our Ground? What more have we to do to prevent Mistake and to silence Clamour, but to insert a proper Explanation of the Meaning of the Subfcription in the Book, wherein the young Men write their Names, and read it to them at their Matriculation.

There is a Queſtion revived, whether the Univerſity has a Power to alter any of its Statutes. I enter not into the Diſpute. But one Obſervation, I think a material one: There is a great Difference betwixt altering Statutes that relate to our own internal Regimen, and Statutes by which we are connected to the Conſtitution in Church or State.

Now what is ſaid on the other Side in Favour of the Alteration?

A Public Attack was made in the Houſe of Commons upon our Subſcription. It had not one Advocate. The Friends, and even the Repreſentatives of the Univerſity gave it up as indefenſible. Our Chancellor intends to recommend an Alteration. The Biſhops concur; and all our Friends are alarmed for the Fate of the Univerſity.

But notwithſtanding all this, under Favour, I will preſume to put the following Queſtions:

Had any of theſe reſpectable Perſonages ſo far conſidered the Matter, as to form to themſelves juſt and adequate Notions of the *Intention* of the Univerſity? Did they not, without farther Reflection, take for granted, that the Subſcription implied a
poſitive

positive Assent to the Truth of the Doctrines contained in the Articles? Must they not be convinced upon mature Consideration, and upon the Evidence produced in the Case, that the University never required any such Thing? Can they blame the University for retaining the antient Test, till stronger Reasons are produced for the Alteration of it, than have yet been laid before them? Ought they to be required to make Innovations, merely in Compliance with the Temper of the Times, when they may be thought incompatible with their Duty, and productive of worse Consequences than they are intended to prevent?

I own myself to be under no Panic at having the Matter brought into Parliament. We shall have an Opportunity given us of making our Plea more Public; and should it not be approved, which is a Supposition I am not willing to make, what have we to apprehend? I cannot believe that the Majority of either House will ever concur in any Project to weaken the *Fences* of our Ecclesiastical Constitution, till they mean to alter it in its *Fundamentals*. When that Day comes, the University must fall with the Church. In the mean Time I rely upon the Legislature for our *Security* as well as *Direction*. It is undoubtedly their Province and not ours to make Alterations, as in their Wisdom they shall

judge

judge proper, (whether we think them for the better or the worse) in Matters wherein the Church of England is as much concerned as the University, Our Obedience is due *in omnibus* LICITIS ET HONESTIS.

Dr. Tot—e.

No. XIII.

Objections to the received Test at Matriculation, impartially stated and examined.

OUR Design is not to controvert, much less to censure, the Opinions of those who have already given the Public Information on the important Subject before us: We are persuaded that all sincerely unite in the same generous Work, *the Investigation of Truth.*—We join in it with Deference and Humility; we respect the Characters of those from whom we happen to dissent; we acknowledge the Weight of their Authorities; but in this Case it must be allowed, *Non tam* Auctoritatis *quam* Rationis *momenta quærenda sunt.*

The Necessity of applying some Criterion at Admission is acknowledged on all Sides: The present Test carries with it the Sanction of Time and respectable Authority; Circumstances of the greatest Weight with the Grave and Thinking. Notwithstanding this, Objections are made to it's Continuance :——It must be confessed they are forcible, have an Air of Candour and Liberality,

Liberality, and therefore deserve our Attention.—The worst Tyranny (say they) is that which is exercised over the Minds of Men; it seems to approach to this when an Acknowledgement of the Truth of Propositions is exacted, from those who are known to be incompetent Judges of them:——Is it not a bad Lesson to inaugurate young Persons with, a strange Salutation at the Threshold of Truth, enlightened Science, and pure Morality, to teach to equivocate, to palliate, to evade, or perhaps to *smother Attention, and comply with Conditions*; Arts which if delivered thus at Matriculation, may perhaps (there are who want not Ill-nature enough for the Suggestion) not be quite useless in some of the Ceremonies at taking Degrees.——Does it not seem a probable Method of depriving young Men of every Religious Principle, or of making them alike indifferent to all, to tempt them thus to hurry over an ill-conceived Assent; to impose on themselves, or accommodate with their Consciences in Matters of such serious Moment?——The Efficacy of the Act of Subscription may indeed be *ingeniously obscured*, but cannot be *fairly* and *conscientiously* misunderstood: If it has *any Meaning*, it amounts to an Acknowledgement of the Truth of those several Propositions to which it is annexed;

ed; of these * several are in their own Nature Metaphysical and recondite Speculations; they are the Conclusions of long and abstruse Reasonings; to require Assent to such from one who is utterly uninformed of the Train of Argument which gave them being, seems like obtruding on the Mind of a Learner the Conclusions of Propositions in the Elements of *Euclid*, as so many *intuitive Truths*. If a Beginner must take some Things upon Trust, and out of Deference to the Authority of his Teacher, let what he receives in this Manner be no more than is necessary to form a Foundation for farther Information; let it be purely *simple* and *elementary*.—" *Sanctius ac reverentius* credere *quam* scire," may be a Maxim in the Mouth of Ignorance and Superstition; and let it be confined to those who profess a Faith that hides itself from Reason.——Notwithstanding the avowed Difference between Faith and Knowledge; who will venture to pronounce *that in any Case* the Mind can give it's Assent to a Proposition without having perceived the Reasons that should influence it, or indeed without *even knowing what that is* to which it's Assent is afforded? Further, it is urged that many of the Articles contain † negative

---

* Such for Instance are the following Articles. (10.) Of Free-Will. (11.) Of Justification. (13.) Of Works before Justification. (17.) Of Predestination and Election.

† Such are implied in Articles 19, 22, 28, 31.

tive Propositions, to be able to assert the Truth of which a *very high Degree of Certainty* is requisite ; and that in general it is expected that this Conviction be extended to them all, that they rest on Scripture as their Foundation.——It is insinuated that although Bishop Burnet is so very *liberal* as to declare * that a Person who conceives some of these Propositions to be erroneous or even false may still *fairly* and *conscientiously* subscribe to them, notwithstanding the useful Art He possessed of reconciling and accommodating such *little Difficulties* to himself, that in *Respect to his Authority with others*,

 † " On sçait fort bien que ses paroles,
 " Ne sont pas *Articles de fois*."

With respect to an explanatory Clause in Nature of Saunderson's *Epinomis*, I have heard it objected, that *a Law indeed* prescribing a Rule of future Conduct, and containing a Sanction, offers an Alternative, " *Observe the Rule, or submit to the* " *Sanction* ;" But that a Declaration of Belief, which confines itself to the present Moment, which carries with it no temporal Sanction, can possibly from it's Nature admit of no candid conscientious Interpretation but this,—" *I assert my present Faith* " *and Conviction in these Matters to be as set* " *forth in the Articles to which I subscribe.*"

What

---

* Exposition of Articles, p. 6. † Boileau.

What Alternative can here be *fairly* intended :—Either I truly declare the State of my Mind, or I impose on the Society of which I am received a Member,—and that *Being alone against whom all Disguise is useless*, can punish my Falsehood and Æquivocation.———But you are to *subscribe* to certain Propositions, *what they mean* you cannot comprehend, this only you are told, that nothing more is inferred from your *Subscription*, than a Promise of *Silence and Acquiescence :*—Can then a Mind totally uninformed acquiesce in Points it is ignorant of ;—is not this very Acquiescence the Consequence of a *Judgement,* " *that the Doc-* " *trines proposed are of such a Nature, that* " *the Mind may approach to Assent, may* " *safely acquiesce and submit ?*"———Suppose (if I may hazard even the Supposition) they contain Assertions inconsistent with the great Principles of *Natural Religion*, would not *blind Acquiescence* be highly culpable ?

After all, why use so *complicated a Machine*, when a very simple one will answer the Purpose ? Is there not great Reason to fear perpetual Misapprehensions,. where an Act in its *Natural Tendency* leads to *one Thing*, but the *Spirit* we are told means somewhat very different ? Is it not *reasonable* that in Matters of the utmost Moment, *Letter and Spirit* should coincide, that the Design of the Legislator should be marked

marked with *as strong and precise a Stroke* as possible?—instead of being left so vague and indefinite as to submit to the Mercy of an *arbitrary Interpretation*, or a *mental Salvo?* Are *Mystery* and *Uncertainty* to be studiously affected in Matters that, of all others, require to be *simple*, *perspicuous*, and *defined?*—Is there here Room even for the *ungenerous* and *pernicious* Distinction, " *Est isthuc quidem* honestum, *verum hoc* " expedit?"—*Quam vero* ILLA AUREA, " *ut inter* BONOS BENE AGIER *oportet!*"—

Such are the Objections to the present Test, either taken in it's Rigour, or *softened* and *accommodated* by a *disarming Clause:*——But it is impossible to substitute one which shall be candid and liberal, not likely on the one Side to become *an Object of Terror*, and to exclude all that have Reflexion and Conscience, until their Scruples have been removed by some ingenious Friend

" *Qui Juris nodos, & Legum ænigmata solvat.*"

Nor yet so *indefinite* and *loose*, as to admit of an Illustration, which by expresly giving up the natural Meaning of the Act, leaves it indeed *totally void of Meaning* or *Obligation:*—Is it in a Word impossible that on this Occasion, the *Maker* of the Rule should be explicit with the *Receiver* of it?—I humbly apprehend, that to act *deliberately* otherwise, would be to endan-
ger

ger the Titles of *Reasonable, Conscientious, Grave, Candid.*—The End in Speculation is the Exclusion of all who *dissent* from the established Church.—The Oath of Supremacy stands on the surest Basis; the *Necessity* of that Test will not I believe easily be questioned, nor can it's *Efficacy* be doubted in the Exclusion of those whom we are bound to guard against with peculiar Caution, the *Votaries of the Church of Rome.* As effectually would a solemn Subscription to the *Declaration of Conformity* operate to preserve us from the Intrusion of Sectaries of every Denomination; it is introduced into this Place under Authority of the Act of Uniformity, which enjoins all Heads and Fellows of Colleges, in Presence of the Vicechancellor, and within *six Months* after their Appointment, to subscribe that Declaration. It is explicit and effectual; it affords no possibility of Mistake, it *requires no Comment.* —— I submit it with Deference, whether it might not be sufficient to enjoin the Tutor before he presents his Pupil to the Vicechancellor, to read over with him the Oath of Supremacy, and this declaratory Form; which should be again solemnly repeated before Subscription *at Matriculation:* ——— Let Subscription to Articles be exacted with that *Caution* and *Tenderness* which the Abstruseness strufeness of the Subject, and a solemn Declaration of *that Faith* which alone admits of *Reason* in her Train, *requires* and *deserves:* let it be expected of those only who can be fairly supposed, whom *alone* the University herself supposes *(vid. Stat. Tit.* 3. §. 2.) capable to judge of the Act they perform:—I would rank under this Head, Candidates for the Degree of Batchelor of Arts *in Orders*, all who offer for that of Master of Arts, and the superior Degrees.

An Alteration in the received Test is not pressed from Fears of temporal Inconveniencies, or an Apprehension of *the Interposition of Parliament*, but from a Persuasion that it is injurious to the Credit of our Body; unworthy the Sanction of Persons of that *enlarged and liberal Way of thinking, which is the best Gift of Erudition*; that it is in its present Form *indefensible* and contrary to the great Principles of *Justice* and *Reason*. Though Parliament were to promise us *Silence* and *Acquiescence*, we shall still be amenable to the Bar of a *Superior Court*, we shall still be liable to the Censures of a Law of a *higher Nature*, of an eternal and *indispensible* Obligation, *Neque enim aut per* Senatum, *aut per* Populum *solvi* HAC LEGE *possumus*.

OXFORD, April, 7, 1772.

No. XIV.

The *plain* and *obvious* Meaning of the received TEST at MATRICULATION, examined and vindicated.

TO remove the Imputation alledged against the University of an arbitrary and illiberal Conduct in requiring from Persons to be matriculated Subscription to the Articles, and to justify the Wisdom and Piety of those, upon whose Authority this Test has been long established, are Ends extremely desirable in themselves, and in the present Juncture of more than ordinary Importance.

The only Plea hitherto suggested, has been the Supposition, that this Subscription was originally intended as a Security for the mere *Acquiescence* of the Subscriber in the Doctrines comprised in those Articles.—A Declaration merely obligatory upon the Will, and in no Degree implying the *Assent* of the Mind to certain Propositions.

The Argument for this Plea is founded upon the following Considerations—" That the Age of the
" Persons subscribing, and the abstruse Nature of the
" Doctrines contained in some of the Articles, leave
" no Room to expect, upon good Grounds, a *rational*
" and *positive* Assent — That the Requisition of such
" Assent is nowhere *expressed* by the Power enjoining
" the Subscription.—That the Persons to be matricu-
" lated are not supposed previously even to have read
" the said Articles; and therefore, in an equitable
" Con-

"Construction of positive Laws, no Confession of Faith, no Limitation of Opinion, can reasonably be deduced by *Implication:* In this Case especially, where the same Persons are required by *express* Injunction at their *second* Subscription, in order to their Degree, to give their *full Assent.* They are moreover obliged to bring Testimony of their having read, or heard others read, these Articles: And that this Assent might be founded on a reasonable and competent Knowledge, the Tutor is admonished by the same Authority diligently to explain them."

"How then shall this Difference in the Mode and Circumstances of the Requisition be accounted for, unless we suppose, that the Tests exacted were essentially different? The one, simple Subscription, implying merely *Acquiescence:* The other a *full and formal Assent* to the Doctrines, *&c.*"

As the Force of the Argument thus stated depends wholly upon the Solution of this Question, we have only to enquire into the Nature and Meaning of the Test in the *first* Instance of Subscription. With respect to the Test in the *second* Instance, it is universally acknowleged to be a full and formal Assent to the xxxix Articles.

The Interpretation of Acquiescence in the *first* Case is certainly to the Generality of the World a *novel* Interpretation of a Test, which has been complied with almost for the Space of *two hundred* Years, and which has not ever been explained in this Manner by the Magistrate, before whom Subscription is made; nor is any Proof offered of its having been the general Sense of the University, at any Period, since the Establishment of the Test.

What was the Sense, in which the Imposers enjoined it to the Kingdom in general, and what Inference they drew from the Compliance with it, we may learn

learn from the Royal Declaration prefixed to the Articles themselves. "Yet we take comfort in "this, that all Clergymen within our Realm have al-"ways most willingly subscribed to the Articles esta-"blished: *Which is an Argument to Us, that they all* "*agree in the true, usual, and literal Meaning of the said* "*Articles.*" The Conclusion made from Subscription is here not the *Acquiescence* of the Party subscribing, but expresly his *actual Agreement*; to the usual Meaning of the said Articles.

In the Title to the Articles their End and Use is set forth, "Ad tollendam *dissentionem*, et *consensum* in vera "religione firmandum;" in the English, "for avoid-"ing DIVERSITIES of Opinions, and for the stablish "ing of *Consent* touching True Religion."

To say the least, the Presumption seems highly improbable, that, so soon * after the End and Use of the Articles had been declared by Authority to be "for avoiding Diversities of Opinions, and for the "stablishing of Consent touching true Religion," the Chancellor and University should enjoin Subscription in a Sense so widely different, and Evade the Force of it by demanding only a *bare Acquiescence.* Some *positive Proof* should be adduced, before this can reasonably be admitted.

The Writer of the "Vindication, &c." is of Opinion, that this Construction is authorised "in Cases "not merely academical." "Simple Subscription is "all that is required for Deacons' Orders, and *need* "imply no more than a mere Acquiescence; but the "Case is different with Respect to a Priest, of whom "positive *Profession* is required—a Testimonial both of "his honest Life and of his *professing* the Doctrine "expressed in the Articles."

* The English Translation of the Articles was confirmed in Convocation in the Year 1571; and Subscription at Matriculation was introduced in 1581.

That, what is here termed simple Subscription in the Case of Deacons *doth* imply more than *mere Acquiescence*, and indeed an *actual Profession* may, I think, be collected from the Royal Declaration, "requiring "*all* our loving Subjects to continue in the uniform "*Profession* of the Articles of the Church of England." This is further confirmed in the first Section of the Ecclesiastical Constitutions published in the Reign of Elizabeth; and yet more expresfsly in the Canons agreed upon in the Reign succeeding. Section 34. "Nullus Episcopus in sacros Ordines quenquam de "cætero cooptabit, qui non ex suâ ipsius Diocesi fue- "rit, nisi, &c." (with certain Exceptions following, to which is added)—"Si *Diaconus* fieri expetit, vice- "simum tertium, sin Presbyter, vicesimum quartum "Annum jam compleverit—vel saltem, nisi *rationem* "*Fidei suæ juxta Articulos Religionis in Synodo Episcopo-* "*rum et Cleri Ann.* 1562 *approbatos Latino Sermone* "*reddere possit,* ·*et eandem Scripturæ testimoniis* CORRO- "BORARE." Here is no Distinction between the Requisites for Deacons' and Priests' Orders, but what arises simply from the different Ages specified.

Upon the whole, I find no Reason to admit a Difference in the *Degrees* of Assent, required at the first and second Subscription in the University; much less to apprehend, that we are justified in explaining this Test in any Case, as a Security for the *Acquiescence only* of the Party subscribing.

The Point remaining is to consider, whether our Ancestors, in imposing Subscription to the Articles upon Persons to be matriculated, in it's *plain and obvious* Sense, and in the Sense in which our University has *hitherto* understood it, have demanded a Test, which may be vindicated upon *fair and equitable* Grounds.

The

The Objection to it rests entirely upon a Supposition, that we cannot with Propriety give our *Assent* to the Truth of Propositions, which we do not fully comprehend. But this is to forget the Distinction between Faith and Knowledge—to forget that Testimony may be a reasonable Ground of Assent as well as Logical Conclusions—that our Assent to many Truths, above the Comprehension of the Age, at which Subscription is made, is required universally at least at as early a Period: Indeed whenever we publickly profess to *believe* the most plain Propositions of Natural and Revealed Religion, the Being of a God and the Necessity of Redemption. At the Time of Confirmation, which usually takes Place before the Parties are brought to the University, they "acknow-
" ledge themselves bound to *believe* all those Things
" which their Godfathers undertook for them" at their Baptism. Much upon the same Principle, it is apprehended, that infinitely the greater Proportion of Mankind *believe* the Truth of every religious Proposition whatever during their whole Lives. If such Assent be not rational, the Faith of that same Proportion of Mankind is void.

" But can the Assent of Persons be honestly given
" to Articles, which they have neither read nor heard
" read?" I answer, They are always apprised (if we except Instances of Neglect) that the Subscription required is to the Truth of the Doctrines of the Church of England in general; which, in the Gross and without Exception, in the Course of their Education they are before taught to *believe* agreeable to the Word of God.

It will be said then that " in Fact they do little more
" in this Test, than declare the Principles of their Pa-
" rents and Instructors." I answer, were *this all*, the End obtained would be by no Means immaterial to the

the Security of our Academical Constitution. But, in Truth, the Supposition, taken in it's Latitude, doth not at all imply, that they are on that Account *incapable* of giving a rational Assent. A full and formal Assent is always just, where Conviction is the Effect of Evidence. It is not essential to the Integrity of such Assent, what may be the Nature of the Means and Motives of Conviction. In *this* Case, the Assent is in great Measure founded upon the Testimony of Persons, in whom they *necessarily* repose the most intire Confidence. In Fact, there is no Impropriety in *assenting* to Points of *mere Opinion*; least of all, when that Opinion is founded upon the mature Conviction of Men respectable for their Numbers, their Learning and Integrity, and whose religious Principles have been confirmed by the Wisdom of Ages. Upon the same Grounds the Legislature have judged it expedient to exact an *Oath* (that of Supremacy) at the Age of Sixteen; when it cannot be thought, that the Parties are assured of it's Fitness purely from their own personal Examination of the Subject-matter. And Courts of Judicature admit the Oath of Persons yet younger, when the very Existence of the Being, whom they adjure, is known to them only by Testimony.

It is not however intended, that, in these Seats of Religion and Learning, our Faith should always rest on the Testimony of our Instructors. Probability in its highest Degrees supposes a Possibility of Error. Matters therefore of Opinion, however plausible, should be carefully weighed and examined in Proportion to the Importance of the Subject. It is a Duty peculiarly incumbent upon us of *this Place* to give every possible Confirmation to the Truth — to add to our *Faith* and Virtue, *Knowledge*. The Statutes of the University have accordingly injoined the Tutors to in-

struct

struck their Pupils particularly in the Rudiments of Religion, and the Articles of the Church; to which, it is expected, they give their Assent in the second Instance of Subscription from a Conviction founded originally in a great Degree upon Testimony, but now confirmed by Knowledge, the Result of due Consideration and Enquiry. Our Church itself hath acted with a similar Precaution, when she hath demanded universally from *all* her Members a *Profession* of her Faith, but from the Clergy in particular an Ability to explain and defend the Reasonableness of her Articles. In fine, I cannot but conclude, that Subscription to the Articles in it's *plain* and *obvious* Notion hath actually been required, and may still continue to be required upon fair and equitable Motives. *Sincerity* lays no Obligation upon us to convert our Articles of Religion into Articles of Peace. *An Acquiescence*, when it falls short of Assent in Matters of Speculation, is not to me intelligible—as a Declaration of the Will, it is merely negative, and by no Means amounts to a Declaration of Conformity.

The Respect due to the World, the Justice due to Ourselves, filial Regard to the Memory of our Ancestors, may render it expedient to explain fully and openly the *true* Motives upon which the University hath demanded Subscription in it's present Mode. At the same Time it were to be wished, that the Nature of our Defence might be as *plain* and *simple* as possible. An *ingenious* Argument carries with it *necessarily* a Degree of Suspicion. The *Prudence of Concessions* will best be measured by the *Value of the Thing ceded*. An honest and upright Justification will at least recommend our Integrity—our Integrity will secure us Favour and Protection.

OXFORD, *April.* 10, 1772.

No. XV.

Subscription at MATRICULA-TION considered, with Respect to the *Nature* of the Act, and the *Extent of it's Obligation*.

THERE are four several States of the Design of Subscription at Matriculation, and of the Extent of it's Obligation; For, it is either

I.—" A Declaration of Belief, and carries with it an unfeigned assent to *all* the Propositions the Articles contain, *grounded on a full and clear Comprehension of their Truth*;" or

II.—" It is nothing more than a Promise of *Silence* and *Acquiescence*, which is sincerely made with respect to *all the Matters comprised in the Articles subscribed to*;" or

III.—" It amounts to a Declaration of *Belief*, and carries with it an unfeigned *Assent* to the Truth of a *few only* of the Articles subscribed, which are distinguished from others by the Title of *Articles of Faith*, and mark out the great Lines of the Christian Scheme;—— With respect to the greater Number, which are called *Articles of Religion*, Subscription operates merely as *a Promise of Silence and Acquiescence*, and carries with it only a *Kind of Negative Engagement*;" or

IV.—" It is a Declaration of *Belief*, and carries with it an *unfeigned Assent* to the Truth of *All* the Propositions contained in the Articles; founded not upon a Comprehension either of their Nature or Meaning, But resting solely on *Deference to Authority*,

rity, and upon the *Testimony* of Persons in whom the Subscribers *necessarily* repose the greatest Confidence:" ———

I. — The Subscription spoken of, " is a Declaration of Belief, and carries with it an unfeigned Assent to *all* the Propositions the Articles contain, *grounded on a full and clear Comprepension of their Truth.*"
— This State of the Case has been abandoned as *unsafe Ground* by the most zealous Defenders of the received Test; We will therefore presume it to be allowed on all Sides, that upon *this Hypothesis* the *Test in Question* is indefensible; *Because* " it is impossible that *Reasonable* Beings can *with Truth* declare their *Assent*, grounded on a *full* and *clear Comprehension* of that, which they have not *examined* or *even heard of*."

II. — Subscription " is nothing more than a Promise of *Silence and Acquiescence*, which is sincerely made with respect to *all the Matters comprised in the Articles subscribed to*."

The ingenious Assertors of this Hypothesis are desired to consider whether the following Objections may not deserve some Attention. ——— It is apprehended that the Difference in the Degrees of Assent required at the *First* and *Second* Subscription remains to be demonstrated: ——— The * *Mandatory* Words of the Law, are exactly the same in both Instances. — So Essential a Distinction would, it is conceived, have been *expressly* and *precisely* marked, and not have been trusted purely to *Implication*: — We have therefore a right to expect some full and positive Proof that such a Difference was meant — 'till this hath been adduced, Presumption is against the Distinction; ——— Because (1) in interpreting a Law the *salutary Purpose* of it, must ever be considered, and, as as far

---

* *Articulis Fidei et Religionis subscribant.* Stat. Tit. 2. § 3. — Tit. 9. §. 3.

the Expressions us'd will bear, it must be so construed as to provide effectually for the *End* in Contemplation of the Legiflator: — The Title of the Articles sufficiently specifies their Object, For they are said to be framed for "*the avoiding Diversities of Opinions, and for establishing Consent touching true Religion;*" The Interpretation here proposed (*of mere Acquiescence and Submission*) it is apprehended disarms the Law, and renders it inadequate to the Purposes for which it was enacted. — Because (2) the Mind of the Legiflator is farther illustrated by this striking Circumstance; Subscription is required of those only who have attained to their *twelfth Year*. —— Now, it is apprehended, that Promises of Silence and Acquiescence may be made by a Boy who can write his Name, as *reasonably* and *effectually* at any Age under *Twelve*, as after he hath arrived at that Period; —— It follows therefore, that the Views of the Legislator were not limited to mere *Submission* and *Forbearance*. — [b] *Acquiescence* in *Matters* of *ordinary Concern* may be defined, "*an accommodating of our Will to that of another Person,*" When referred to Points of Speculation, the only Meaning it can have, is, that the Mind engages to withhold itself from considering certain Propositions; — Keeps itself *suspended and in equipoise* — if it *incline* ever so little on either side, it *ceases* to *acquiesce*, it *begins* to *assent* or *deny*: — As to myself, I own I can by no Means conceive how the Mind can possibly be said to *acquiesce* (*i. e.* as far as *acquiescing* is distinguished from *assenting* or *dissenting*) in Points merely Speculative; For the Mind either *considers* these Propositions, or it doth *not consider them*; —— If it *considers* them, it must *form some Opinion about them*, and therefore *cease* to be merely *passive* and *indolent*,

---

[b] The Term *Acquiescence* is made use of merely to evade the Objections that immediately oppose themselves to the Expression "*Full and unfeigned Assent;*" And is therefore fairly considered as purposely contradistinguished.

or *quiescent*; if it *does not consider* them, it cannot be said *to acquiesce* with respect to *these Propositions in particular*, inasmuch as it doth not *at all know what they are*.

III. Subscription amounts to a Declaration of *Belief*, and carries with it an unfeigned *Assent* to the Truth of a *few only* of the Articles subscribed, which are distinguished from the others by the Title of *Articles of Faith*, and mark out the great Lines of the Christian Scheme; —— With respect to the greater Number, which are called *Articles of Religion*, Subscription operates merely as *a Promise of Silence* and *Acquiescence*, and carries with it only a *Kind of Negative Engagement*."

That such would have been the Decision of Bp *Conybeare*, as to the Nature and Extent of the Obligation incurred by the Subscription spoken of, we may fairly collect from what he says in general of the Subscriptions of the *Laity*, ᶜ "the Distinction between Articles of *Faith* and Articles of *Religion (says he)* is suggested in the very Title of the Articles; Articles of *Faith* consist only of such Truths as are *Fundamental* in the Christian Scheme; By Articles of *Religion* we understand such Truths as being founded in Scripture have a certain Evidence, but not bearing so close and immediate a Relation to the *Main* Branches of the Christian Scheme, are therefore of an inferior Nature;—Having noted this, I am led on to observe farther, that as there is in the Reason of Things, a considerable Difference between the Case of the *Clergy* and of the *Laity*, so the Wisdom of the Church hath carefully preserved this Difference in relation to *Subscriptions*. The latter merely considered as Christians, are required to profess their Belief of the *fundamental* Articles of our Faith,—other Doctrines, as

---

ᶜ Sermon on the Case of Subscription to the Articles of Religion: Aº. 1725. p. 6. 7.

not being the *distinguishing* and *essential* Marks of a Christian are less necessary to be *distinctly* understood, and *explicitly professed* by them." —— The Influence of this great Authority is, it must be owned, much weak'ned by what the same Person adds almost immediately, where I desire it may be considered whether, the *fair Meaning, and virtual Obligation* of the Act of Subscription taken *Simply* and *in itself* be not spoken of: [d] "One Thing yet remains in order to the full State of this Subject; and that is to consider, what is implied in the *Subscription itself*; Whether it expresses our *Assent* to the Truth of the Articles subscribed, or be only an Engagement not to *dispute* or *contradict* them: I conceive it will appear that our Subscrption amounts to an *Approbation of, and Assent to,* the Truth of the Doctrines subscribed; and that, *First,* Because this seems to be implied in the bare *Act of Subscribing*; and we should be understood, by every indifferent Spectator, as *approving* the Truth of those Doctrines, unless the *Form of Subscription* declared the contrary; nor would any one be apt to consider them as *Articles of Peace,* but as *Articles of Doctrine.* This Notion is farther confirmed by the very *Title* of the Articles themselves; For they are said to be framed, for *the avoiding Diversities of Opinions, and for establishing Consent touching true Religion:* But this End cannot be obtained, unless they are subscrib'd as *Truths assented to.*" —— It does not appear an easy Undertaking to reconcile these two Opinions; — The latter strongly opposes the present Hypothesis, which is by no means admissible; Because (1) It is impossible that the *same undivided* Act should superinduce *various Obligations* on the *same* Person, with respect to the *same Object*; (2) The Line between those Doctrines which are considered as *Points of Faith,* and *fundamental,* and

[d] Ib. p. 9. 10.

such

such as are said to be of an *inferior Nature*, and less necessary to be *distinctly understood*, or *explicitly expressed*, is no where drawn; How then is the young Person who subscribes enabled to say, "here, *reasonable Belief and full Assent* leave off," Here, *Promises of Forbearance and Acquiescence* begin? — Because (3) It is evident that this is a mixed Kind of Defence, partaking in a great Measure of the *first* and *second States*, so that, besides Objections which are *peculiar*, several of those mention'd in the *first* and *second* Cases, point likewise against this. —— But to consider the *last Hypothesis*;

IV. Subscription "is a Declaration of *Belief*, and carries with it an *unfeigned Assent* to the Truth of *All* the Propositions contained in the Articles, founded not upon a Comprehension either of their Nature or Meaning; But resting solely on *Deference to Authority*, and upon the *Testimony* of Persons in whom the Subscribers *necessarily* repose the greatest Confidence." ——

First then, here is a *full and express Assent* and *Declaration of Belief* spoken of, this Case therefore may be reduced to the *first Head*, and is equally indefensible; "Because it is impossible that *reasonable* Beings, can upon *any motives*, *with Truth* declare their Assent to that which they have *not examined*, or *even heard of*." — The Author of a Paper entitled, "*The plain and obvious Meaning*," &c. who defends this Ground with some Degree of Ingenuity, has yet fallen into a strange Contradiction; which is indeed the Basis of his whole Performance: "Upon the whole (says He) I find no Reason to admit of *any Difference* in the *Degrees* of *Assent* required at the *first* and *second* Subscription in the University; — In the Case of the *first*, the Assent is founded upon the Testimony of Persons in whom the Subscribers *necessarily* repose the most entire Confidence: — But it is not intended that in these Seats of Religion and
Learning

Learning our Faith should always rest on the Testimony of our Instructors, it is a Duty peculiarly incumbent upon us of this Place, to give every possible Confirmation to the Truth, to add to our *Faith* and *Virtue, Knowledge*; The Statutes of the University have accordingly enjoined the Tutors to instruct their Pupils particularly in the Rudiments of Religion, and the Articles of the Church, to which it is expected they give their Assent in the *second Instance* of *Subscription* from a Conviction founded *originally upon Testimony*, but *now* confirmed by *Knowledge* the *Result of due Consideration and Enquiry.*" It is submitted to the *Candour* and *better Judgement* of this Writer, whether there be not a very *essential Difference* between the *Degree* of *Assent* afforded, upon *mere Testimony*, and *rested on the Judgment and Opinion of others*, to Articles which have *neither been read or heard read*, and *That*, given to the same, upon a full *Comprehension of their Meaning* and *a Knowledge of their Truth*, the Result of due *Consideration* and *Enquiry:* ——— Let us however farther examine whether the Ground of Defence here chosen be tenable or no: The Author of the Paper referred to tells us, " That young Persons may *honestly* give their *Assent* to Articles which they have *neither read*, or *heard read*; They know in general their Tendency, and *assent to them in the Gross* upon the Authority of their Parents and Instructors." To confirm this he assures us that, *Testimony* may be a *reasonable* Ground of Assent, as well as *logical Conlusions:* ——— Though this be allowed, and I believe it will not be disputed, much is wanting to *prove* that an Assent afforded in the Manner spoken of, can be (as he repeatedly terms it) *rational* and *upon Conviction:* ——— Let us for a Moment consider the Definition of *reasonable Assent in Matters of Faith*: " There is one Sort of Propositions (says *Mr. *Locke*) that chal-

---

* Essay—b. 4. c. 16. §. 14.— c. 17. §. 24.— c. 18. §. 10.—
lenge

lenge the highest Degree of our Assent upon bare Testimony; The Reason whereof is because the Testimony is of such an one as cannot deceive nor be deceived, and that is of God himself: —This (Testimony) is called by a peculiar Name *Revelation*, and our Assent to it *Faith*, — But whether it be a *divine Revelation* or no, *Reason* must judge; — Faith if it be regulated as is our Duty, *cannot be afforded* to any Thing but upon *good Reasons*:" ——— But the Assent which follows the Testimony of Parents and Instructors is notwithstanding declared to be *full, honest* and *reasonable* although it comes from those who are *totally uninformed* not only *why* they profess such *Assent*, but who have *neither read, nor heard read, that* which they assent to: may not it be fairly asked, whether the proper Object of such *reasonable Assent* be not rather the Miracles of the *Legende dorée* or *Fleur des Saints*, than the Articles of a Church famous for her Wisdom, Justice, Candour and Moderation? — I beg Leave to put one Assertion of this Writer's, already touched on, in a still stronger Light: He declares that, "it is not essential to the Integrity of Assent given to Evidence, what may be the Nature of the *Means and Motives* of Conviction;" Conviction therefore, may be as *reasonable* and *compleat* upon the *weakest* and *worst-conceived Evidence*, as upon the *fullest*, the *clearest*, and least *exceptionable* the case can admit of; There are then, no different Degrees and Grounds of Probability; No Difference between the various Shades of *Conjecture, Opinion, Persuasion, Belief; Knowledge* "*the Result of due Consideration and Enquiry*" can add no Confirmation to the Truth; there is, in a Word, no Difference between *reasonable Faith*, and a *blind Opinion* that there are certain Propositions which *others understand and believe*, and the Truth of which they would have us accede to, altho' what *these are*, or upon *what Grounds* they merit to be received, are Points that remain to *Us* alike involved

volved in *Myſtery* and *Obſcurity*: — An Acknowledgement of the Truth of Propoſitions, where no *Evidence* on which ſuch Profeſſion ſhould be founded has been *diſcovered* or *examined*, where the Propoſitions *themſelves are not underſtood*, and *have not even been read*, cannot be ſtiled a *reaſonable*, *honeſt Aſſent*, but muſt be referred to *Weakneſs* or *Prejudice*; It is *idle* if not *unjuſt* to exact ſuch an Acknowledgement, it is *inconſiderate* if not *Diſhoneſt* to make it.

Such are the moſt material Objections to each particular Hypotheſis; A Preſumption unfavourable to them all, it muſt be acknowledged, ariſes from hence, that in the Place where this Teſt hath ſo long obtained, the very Perſons who have required it, and who continue to patronize it, are not only *not agreed* what *Mode* of *Defence* they may rely on, but ſeem even at a loſs *what Interpretation* they ſhall give to an Act, whoſe *full and Natural* Obligation they are afraid to avow.

Oxford, *April* 18. 1772.

AN APPENDIX

TO THE

COLLECTION, &c.

THE Defence of the prefent Mode of Subfcription refts upon one clear Point, plain and intelligible to all Capacities. The Speculations and Refinements of Mr. *Locke* and *Bifhop Conybeare* have nothing to do in the Cafe. It offers itfelf to the Underftanding of the *Illiterate,* but does not decline the fevereft Scrutiny of *Logical and Theological Learning.* To explain it once more, it is this:

Every true Member of the Church of England is fuppofed to acquiefce in the Doctrines of it upon this Principle, that he *believes* it does not maintain any Doctrines contrary to the Chriftian Faith into which he has been baptized, whether he underftands them or not. The Univerfity requires a Subfcription to thefe Doctrines from all Scholars at their Matriculation,

lation, as a Teſt that they are actual Members of the Church of England, the Conſtitution of the Univerſity requiring them to admit *no other*. It requires this Subſcription, not as a poſitive Aſſent, upon *real Knowledge and Conviction*, to the Truth of the Doctrines, but as an *Acquieſcence in them*, or in other Words, *as a Declaration that they are perſuaded, and have no Suſpicions to the contrary, that the Church, of which they declare themſelves to be Members, does not maintain any falſe Doctrines contrary to the true Faith of a Chriſtian*. It has been proved beyond Contradiction, that the Univerſity requires nothing more: This it has a Right to require, and no *real Member* of the Church of England can have the leaſt Scruple in making this Declaration.

Agreeably to this, ſuppoſe that ſome ſuch Form as the following one ſhould be read by every Scholar at his Matriculation: " I A. B.
" do declare, by this my Subſcription, that
" I profeſs myſelf to be a Member of the
" Church of England as by Law eſtabliſhed;
" that I will conform to its Worſhip; and
" that I acquieſce in and receive its Doctrines,
" ſo far as a Belief and Perſuaſion, that the
" Church of England does not hold any Doc-
" trines contrary to the true Faith of a Chriſ-
" tian, will warrant me. And I do promiſe,
" that I will endeavour, in the Courſe of my
" Studies, and with the Aſſiſtance of my
" Tutor, to underſtand the Doctrines of the
" ſaid

"said Church, as they are set forth in the Thirty-nine Articles."

That the University has a Right to require this Subscription, under the Explanation of it here given, and to give it this Explanation, may be confirmed (if it wanted any Confirmation) by the Authority of the Legislature itself, which in the *Oath of Supremacy* proceeds upon the same Grounds. Suppose this Oath to require no more than a bare Renunciation of the Pope's Authority, yet this must be supposed to be made, for the most Part at least, upon the Evidence of *Faith*, not of *Knowledge*; as it is required from all Scholars upon Foundations of eighteen Years of Age; very few of whom can possibly know the Insufficiency of the Grounds of a Claim admitted by one half of Christendom. But, in Truth, the Oath has always been understood by the Legislature to imply *the Supremacy of the King in all Matters ecclesiastical and spiritual*; a Claim erected upon the Downfall of the Pope's Usurpation. And can the young People who are required to take this Oath, be supposed to know, with any Degree of Precision, *what this Supremacy is*, upon what *Right* it is established, and in what *Manner and Cases* it is to be exercised? Certainly not. And yet they are obliged by a Law made 25 Charles II. and confirmed so lately as 9 Geo. II. to receive this Doctrine, and to acknowledge it upon Oath. Upon what Motives? Evidently upon the *Credit* given to the Reformation, and upon a *Presumption*,

sumption, that the Legislature did very right in acting upon the Principles of it, by requiring a Renunciation of the Pope's, and an Acknowledgment of the King's Supremacy.

With what Consistency then, and *upon what Motives*, can the Legislature abrogate the University-subscription, and retain the strongest of all Declarations and Obligations, precisely under the same Circumstances. The University itself surely ought not to do it: It will imply a Condemnation of a long-established Practice; will throw an invidious Imputation upon the Memory of those whom we ought to revere, and bring the Reproach of having continued an unwarrantable Practice upon Ourselves. And for what Reason? Merely to humour the Sceptical Notions and Projects of the Times; and so to bring a Suspicion upon the Doctrines of the Church of England, and to make an Opening for a stronger Attack upon them, which may end in the Destruction of our present Establishment; and all this, under Pretence of *relieving* Consciences which are not *aggrieved*.

F I N I S.

www.ingramcontent.com/pod-product-compliance
Lightning Source LLC
Chambersburg PA
CBHW022138160426
43197CB00009B/1346